LANDSCAPE AND EXILE

edited by
Marguerite Guzman Bouvard

Rowan Tree Press
Boston, Massachusetts

ACKNOWLEDGEMENTS

"Requiem" appeared in the OHIO JOURNAL and "Karel" appeared in the GREENFIELD REVIEW; "A Hundred Tongues" and "A Spring of Quiet and Peace" appeared in the VIETNAM FORUM, (Winter-Spring, 1983); Yuan Chen Variations, by F. T. Prince, copyright, the Sheep Meadow Press, 1981; poems by Denis Brutus appeared in "A Simple Lust," Hill & Wang, 1973, copyright and permission by Denis Brutus; poems by Armando Valladares, copyright and permission by Marta and Armando Valladares; "The Exile" appeared in the MASSACHUSETTS REVIEW in 1970; "The Cross" appeared in Diacoute 1, "Shoushoun," in Diacoute 11, "Dream" in Diacoute 111, and "Boat People" in Diacoute 1, 11, 111, copyright and permission by Felix Morrisseau-Leroy; "Kindergarten" appeared in "Kindergarten," Houghton Mifflin, 1970, copyright and permission by Elzvieta Ettinger; "On the Continental Divide," "Memento", "Where the Cloister Stood," "Creatures of Land and Water," appeared in "From the Hungarian Revolution: Poems," edited by David Ray, Cornell University Press, 1966, copyright, Tibor Tollas; "Summer's End," and "The Trees in My Orchard," appeared in "Jrgalmas Fak," Nemzetor, Munich, 1975; "In the Whirlwind," "Prayer for a Peaceful Death," "Caracas," and "The Bend in the River Danube," appeared in "Forgo-Szelbev," Nemzetor, Munich, 1983, copyright Tibor Tollas; "You Can't Get From Here to There," appeared in STORY, 1982; "On Dostoevsky Street," appeared in PEQUOD, 1983; "Ezidimma," appeared in PLOUGHSHARES, vol. 7, no. 1, 1981; "The Long Journeys," appeared in THE SOUTHWEST REVIEW, vol. 80, 1972; "To You," "The Apricot Tree," "Epigrams," "Without Memories," "Oath to Arrarat," "Let It be Light," appeared in "Anthology of Armenian Poetry," edited by Diana Der Hovanessian and Marzbed Margossian, Columbia University Press, copyright Diana Der Hovanessian; "Four Prisoners of War," copyright, Stratis Haviaras.

With grateful acknowledgement to Ana Aloma Velilla, Lily Farkas and Elzbieta Chodakowska.

Cover design by Lazarillo

Rowan Tree Press
124 Chestnut Street
Boston, Massachusetts 02108

TABLE OF CONTENTS

Foreword

The phenomenon of exile is as old as human history, but the uniqueness of exile today lies in its sheer scope and numbers. The recent decades will go down in history as the period when national political turmoil and ideological oppression swelled the population of exiles to inordinate proportions. Under dictatorial political systems, the writer whose function it is to hold up a mirror to society, may find herself or himself silenced, censored or imprisoned because her or his work offends the powers that be. Often, the government will prefer to exile the dissenting writer, thus ridding itself of a potential hero.

The forms of political oppression today are as varied as ideology and therefore, the writers represented in this book come from all parts of the globe: Southeast Asia, Northwest Asia, Africa, the Caribbean, Central Europe, and the Soviet Union. For these men and women, survival has a double meaning. Raymond Aron, the great French sociologist, distinguished between physical death and the death of culture. One can survive war and prison only to be forced into exile, leaving one's culture behind. The issue is a poignant one for the writer who responds to the peculiarity of language, landscape, and society. Language is the ultimate carrier of the culture and of the soul of a people. It contains a way of seeing, of connecting with others. Preserving this culture presents the exiled writer with a dilemma. On the one hand, he or she can seek to maintain his culture, and his past by surrounding himself with members of his own community within the larger society of his exile. He then suffers isolation from the larger society. Or he can attempt to enter that society wholeheartedly only to find himself alienated from his native culture.

In some instances, the writer may revel in political freedom in a new land, only to find himself unable to write. Add to this, the difficulties of a new language. A writer must find translators for his work and in translation, there is an unavoidable loss of music and cadence, of the richness of contemporary idiom, whether Russian or Vietnamese. Many of the writers in this volume have begun a new phase in their literary careers, writing in English instead of Greek, Farsi, Polish, Russian or Nigerian.

The very word exile conjures up a state of anguish. However, the shock of change can also awaken insight. The writer, as an outsider, has a clear vision of his own native land and also of his new society. The price may be a high one, but she or he gains a perspective on life unavailable to those on the inside. Often it is when we journey that we see the most clearly, both the places we have left, and the new and strange places of arrival. Moving between these visions, the writer experiences a unique sense of freedom.

The focus of these collected works is on landscape because it is landscape which nourishes the soul of a writer and which inspires his or her art. We take the trees, fields, and streets that surround us as givens until we are torn from them. Then we feel dismembered. The poignant image of the key dangling from a man's neck in Võ Phiến's story dramatizes this feeling. For each of these writers, landscape is the container of childhood, and in losing this, the writer loses a part of his or her being. This, then is the function of poetry, to nail down each root, plank, and cobblestone of the past, to make an eternity of place. Tibor Tollas returns to the orchards of his childhood from his current home in Munich. Valladares writes of his mountains from his prison cell, and Denis Brutus remembers his "hill and huts, aloes and gray-green dreaming firs." These now, are not only places they can return to again and again, but countries we also can journey to.

In the landscape of the present, the writer recreates a sense of place, makes a universe out of a dark corner. Valladares' prison cell becomes a trysting place. Tollas's cell at Vac prison is once more a medieval cloister with monks weeding the rose beds. For Ezlbieta Ettinger, the sewer is an escape route from the Ghetto where acts of heroism occur. In the most ordinary settings, such as Võ Phiến's shower, life's drama unfolds with all its poignancy. Art serves a very important purpose in today's turbulent world. Under the most brutal conditions, it flames as the purest expression of our humanity.

Poetry and fiction are also the clearest reflection of culture. The peculiarities of syntax, cadence and imagery preserve the unique heritage of a people. Yet while they contain the distinctiveness of landscape and societies, they also uphold a universality in which we can all see ourselves. One feels with Morriseau-Leroy the ironies of myths which exclude us, or with Ludmilla Shtern, the stupidities of officialdom. Always, the writer sees with unflagging vision, women and men as they are, and who they can become. This is ultimately the vision that nourishes us all.

Marguerite G. Bouvard

A Hundred Tongues

Born somewhere, scattered out to the four winds,
a hundred children will speak a hundred tongues.
Tomorrow, if we all should go back home,
let's hope we'll speak the common speech of tears.

Vien Linh, translated from the Vietnamese by
Huynh Sanh Thong

Crane

Where do you come from, crane?
I ache to hear your call,
to know you have come home.
Do you have any news at all?

I bless your wings, your eyes.
My heart is torn in two;
the exile's soul is all sighs
waiting for bits of news.

Excerpt from an Armenian folk song attributed to
Nahabet Koutchag, 12th century troubadour,
translated by Diana Der Hovanessian

The Yuan Chen Variations

You wrote by candle-light
an exile's heartaches-
worst, that the road he takes
lacks friends: and ten
verses with moon, flower, midnight
said it again.

Translated by F. T. Prince

A Spring of Quiet and Peace

Võ Phiến
Translated by Huỳnh San Thông

Back home, the region where I came from knew harsh winters, not because of the cold but because of typhoons and floods. A year seldom went by in Central Vietnam that there didn't happen some natural catastrophe, great or small.

Still, toward the later part of the tenth moon, we all could usually set our fears at rest. Our ancestors had expressly warned us to beware the twenty-third day of the tenth moon. A couplet of folk verse says: "The god spares you, but the goddess will not:/ upon you she will wreak a storm on the twenty-third of the tenth moon." (*Ông tha bà lại không tha, /giáng cho mộ trận hăm ba tháng mười.*) And that was all. Thereafter, we might stop worrying and start thinking a little of spring and its pleasures.

In my memories of childhood in the countryside, spring celebrations are closely linked to the peanut-husking bee. There, people used to sow and plant peanuts during the twelfth moon. Whenever adults in the family gathered to shell peanuts for seed, the children had cause to rejoice and turn their thoughts to Tết (or Vietnamese New Year's). For that reason, the mere act of husking peanuts already hinted a festive mood.

As the nuts were scooped out of the bin into baskets for distribution, every person in the family, old or young, got a share. Someone would lie down in a hammock and shell the nuts swinging to and fro. Someone else would carry the basket out into the garden and find a cool nook where he or she might do the husking and softly sing, letting the mind wander in pursuit of romance. Elderly folks would pop

1

open the nuts and at the same time brood over some past sorrows which, their devastating force spent, rankled still. Children would huddle in some corner of the courtyard to perform their chore while heatedly discussing plans for fun and games. To one and all, the crackle and sputter of peanut husks being crushed echoed inklings of exhilaration within the bosom of a whole family at work.

One and all must pitch in because the task needed to be done in hot haste. Some years we had to sow and plant peanuts until the afternoon of the twenty-ninth, or even until the thirtieth, New Year's Eve. The crackle of peanuts popping open went on and on relentlessly right up to the Nguyên-đán festivities. To shell peanuts was to clear the way for Tết: unless we worked with nimble hands and in concert, the job might not get wrapped up in time. The sputter of peanut shells being broken led straight to the crepitation of firecrackers. Such was the fun of husking peanuts.

We sowed and planted peanuts in dry soil. Likewise, we could set up huts and play the card game called *bài chòi* only out in the open during a warm and dry season. Thus, toward the end of the twelfth moon in my native region, we already enjoyed the atmosphere of spring.

✼

After half a lifetime in such a climate, this year I suddenly found myself celebrating my first Tết in the northern part of the United States of America with about half a meter of snow on my front steps and a cold of some twenty-five degrees C. below zero.

For two months and a half, I had not seen one single drop of water in the liquid state outdoors. I had to wait another two weeks before I got a shower of rain. If God cares to let

2

fall liquid water, it is an effort in the right direction, I gladly told myself. But all that the whole effort amounted to was one splash of rain. Then, a pall of snow and ice all over again.

January had passed by without a sign of spring anywhere. Such rotten business, this! It simply would not do to have no Tết. I had just left my country: how could I forget one of its old customs? But if I was to celebrate Nguyên-đán amidst the dismal gloom of winter, amidst the death and decay of all vegetation beneath that bleak sky, would I not be mocking the idea of renewal, of fresh start, that this one national holiday implies?

On the twentieth of March, I overheard joyous rumors proclaimed all around me that spring was about to spring. In fact, it sprang only on the calendar. Snow refused to budge and melt until the bitter end of the month.

And would I dare to rest easier seeing snow melt? At night, the temperature stayed around freezing point, and in early May a storm dumped a lot of snow, dragging on all day.

The solar month of May meant that it was already the fourth moon. To rephrase a line in *The Tale of Kiều* by Nguyễn Du, the gentleman from Tiên-điên, "of ninety vernal days . . . ninety had fled"! How much longer would I have to wait before I'd be granted a glimpse of spring, O God?

Not only humans (and refugees in particular), but all grasses and plants seemed to be burning with impatience. By no means could they fling forth their leaves and their flowers from beneath the snow. Nevertheless, they made feverish, all-out preparations: the tip of each twig held ready a bud that had appeared God knows since when. From dwarf bushes along the hedges to giant trees beside the roads, on the hills, in the woods, all were on the alert.

Leaf buds kept growing fatter day by day, then swelled out, then sprouted forth. No longer could they afford to wait. They were like drops of water precariously perched on the tips of straws along a thatch roof, like drops of coffee tremblingly poised beneath a filter, about to fall at any moment.

Was it because they had had to wait in a prolonged state of pent-up energy that the leaves and flowers of this country burst forth with such spectacular zest in a jostling, grabbing free-for-all? After barely a few days of warm weather, the leaf buds would peep out early in the week. By the week's end you could see bright green trees, and when another week came around, the whole city was a mass of luxuriant vegetation. The flowers would rush into bloom only to wilt quickly. As soon as snow had melted away, along the wall you could detect a bit of green leaves snooping there as if they had been lurking in wait for some time. Then, while you were not paying attention, one morning out of nowhere tiny violet and yellow flowers had shot up pell-mell. Upon inquiry, they turned out to be Johnny-jump-ups. What a darling of a name! Little naughty boys who would up and romp and then, presto, vanish. A week or ten days later, around the wall tulips would flaunt their gorgeous hues.

Along hedges, in public parks, on the skirts of woods, often could be found trees that were not quite tall and yet had a lush foliage and flowers aglow with a radiant pink. Amidst the grove of light or dark green shrubs and trees, they struck a different, eye-catching note—they cast shimmering reflections in the lake and conjured up the image of cherry blossoms as they kindled a patch of the world. Regrettably, those resplendent flowers were nothing but

4

"crab" apple blossoms. Crabs and turtles do not evoke dignity and "class" in the mind of an average Vietnamese. What name should I give those flowers as a consolation prize? How about *Cancri rosei*?

Cancri rosei staged their show for a week or two, then folded and sank away. Now came the turn of the lilac, apparently. Though associated with the color lilac, its flowers could be violet, or white, or pale blue. The leaves reminded me of those of the bougainvillea (*bông giây*) back home, and the flowers also featured a variety of colors like the bougainvillea. Once lilacs were gone, the hedges displayed a white dazzle of spireas dancing in the wind.

Wave after wave, all those flowers came and went, pushing and crowding one another, chasing one another through a hurry-scurry performance. No, indeed, there was no time for loitering about, was there?

As I passed through the park in front of the Fine Arts School, I stopped short, stunned by the sight of co-eds lying on the lawn in positions that no Vietnamese girl could get away with in public. Those students wanted each and every part of their bodies to drink in sunshine, the warm, precious-as-gold sunshine they had missed for the past six months.

Back at my place, while in my mind still lingered traces of annoyance at the scene I had just witnessed, I raised the window curtain for light and . . . lo and behold! Through the window frame, looking across to the neighbors' house, I saw a girl who was virtually mother-naked, lying all exposed there and sunning herself . . . on the rooftop.

The two- or three-storied houses in the area had small terraces protruding from the roofs. So the girl had spread out her blanket, stripped off her clothes to let every pore absorb sunshine for hours and hours, some ten meters above the ground: no one in the entire neighborhood could have failed to see her. A striped cat was hovering around her, and on the canopy of a nearby elm a squirrel was hopping from branch to branch.

Well, the more radiant the sunshine the more exposure was called for. They would roll out their blankets, haul their cots or mattresses to their gardens, to the lawns in front of their houses, to lake beaches, to hillsides. Then, off went their clothes and they exposed themselves.

I thought of that day when an American visitor had caught me at home in my *bà-ba* suit, mistaken it for a pair of pajamas and betrayed discomfort about it. Indoors, you hermetically dress yourself from neck to foot and may thus commit a breach of etiquette; in public, you nearly reveal your all and fulfill the rules of decorum. In those wrangles over differences between cultures, there are some weird paradoxes.

*

Halfway through life, here I was stranded and lost in an alien, faraway spot of the world, greeting a Tết that was no longer Tết. On the other hand, I am enjoying a belated but truly glorious spring.

Because it arrives late amidst fervent expectations, after a season of raw cold, spring bubbles all the more with spirits, makes people all the drunker, makes their heads spin faster.

Everybody treasures each ray of sunshine. The young, outside of work or study hours, will pour in streams to sports fields, rivers and lakes, hills and brooks. If people don't play ball or row boats, they fish. Some will drive their cars over hundreds of miles to fish. Some will book passage and fly all the way to Canada to fish (although this state,

Minnesota, boasts more than ten thousand lakes). Their fishing done, they will either unhook the fishes caught and toss them back into the water right there and then or bring them home to their friends. They fish for sport, not for food. They fish for an excuse to be on the go, to run from lakes to streams. When the sun shines and warms, they suddenly feel they need a reason to tear about, that's all. As for the old folks who cannot scurry around, they too will get out of their old-age homes in droves. Those who still stand on their own feet volunteer to push the wheelchairs of the palsied and the crippled. One after another, they stroll here and there, parading from street to street.

Why, God is no niggard after all. If you like sunshine, you'll get enough of it to warm the cockles of your heart. By half past five the sun is already up, which means that as of five o'clock the horizon glows. And it is almost nine in the evening before the sun will go down. At eight-thirty p.m., a few diligent blackbirds are still foraging on the front lawn.

God has lavished sixteen hours of sunlight on man. As someone from the tropics, I don't care for sunbathing. Unlike the milk-white beauties of this country, I lack such endowments as warrant exhibition. But still, I cannot resign myself to staying cooped up indoors in a balmy season like this. All day I rove and ramble, tarrying near streams and, tired, sitting down in the shade of a tree, eyes half-shut.

The gentleman from Tiên-điến loved those maple tree colors in autumn, colors connoting "passes and mountains" (*quan-san*), separation and sorrow. His great prestige has caused people to give short shrift to maples in spring. Actually, the hues of the red maple in April, though they do not evoke "passes and mountains", are quite interesting. The flowers are a pale yellow, the leaves are a dark, sharp red, and the flowers outnumber the leaves. Then, in due

7

course, the foliage will grow thicker and slowly turn green while the flowers will fade away. By mid-May, standing amidst other trees with its noble mane of leaves and its myriad keys or double-winged seeds, the maple still keeps a presence all its own, bearing no likeness to anything else.

Like the gentleman from Tiên-điến who preferred autumn, the poet Li Po favored autumn leaves:

> At dawn set sail and go away.
> Down fall and fall the maple leaves.
>
> *(Minh triêu quải phạm khử.*
> *Phong diệp lạc phân phân.)*

Let's suppose Li did not sail down a river in fall but, instead, on a spring day and, after a binge, he found himself slumbering in the shade of a tree on some hilltop. A cool breeze woke him up, and he opened wide his eyes to the sight of maple keys or myriad dried wings swirling and swirling on the wind, scattering through the air. I believe that Li himself would not deem the scene beneath his notice.

The whirligig of maple keys is a space festival—it is the sun and the wind making whoopee in the air. In this Water City, Minneapolis, where in vain have I waited nine months for glimpses of a single butterfly, what will set space astir, make it come to life, if there is no flutter of maple wings?

To Li Po I have just suggested a lazy way to enjoy spring that may irk the action-bent American. Speaking for myself, I must confess that the hours of slothful daydreaming on the grass, under a tree, are those I have relished the most this spring, the first spring of a life in exile.

After last year's psychic shocks, after a claustrophobic winter that just ended, I keep wandering back and forth in the sunshine, my wits still dazed, like a sick man recently up and about. But all my senses are thrilled by a fantastic, eerie world.

This country is so beautiful, so tranquil, so happy. At times, while I watch sunshine play on the leaves or gleam in the water, while I listen to a chorus of songbirds, I catch myself thinking with a jolt: "Hey! But isn't this the most peaceful spring you've known for thirty years?"

Perfect peace, indeed. As I was growing up in my homeland, was there ever any time like this year when I was allowed to hail spring without a worry about offensives and counteroffensives, plans and programs, strategies and "high points", about some drama, political, economic or military, brewing offstage? Now, I am absolutely . . . safe!

From now on, spring will no longer have anything to do with peanuts, nor with policies, plans, high points. What will it mean? Johnny-jump-ups? Sunbathing? Crab apple blossoms? I don't know. At least, all these things will bring on no tragedy, no grief.

My country has chosen to tread paths of woe and heartbreak and is doomed to keep walking down such paths. This spring, next spring, and for many more springs, my compatriots back home will have to struggle with soul-boggling anxieties: revolts, crackdowns, purges, rectifications, policy shifts, emulation drives, leaps forward . . . But personally, I have been cast out of that sphere. From now on, I am to know only springs of quiet and peace. I'll know quiet and peace, but I'll be smarting and hurting.

As all this dawns on you, life abruptly turns into a yawning void. A dreadful, horrible void. Of a sudden, there is nothing left that your eyes can look forward to: you stand utterly outside the circle of all cares and concerns. Good God, the quiet and peace of lives without a future.

9

Spring sunshine in all its glory makes you dizzier, makes your head reel more. Without wings, you feel as if you were swirling and swirling through space, like a maple key in mid-air.

The Key

Võ Phiến

Translated by Phan Phan

To say that the first picture in the memories of the wanderings of an unfortunate man who has lost his country and left everything behind is a shower seems ridiculous. What a strange recollection. Perhaps I should say something sorrowful, more poetic. But how can I? None could take refuge the way he wished.

We came to U.S. territory at night. Despite our excited state, darkness prohibited a clear view of part of a country we were going to spend the rest of our life in. At that late hour the island of Guam seemed to consist of thousands of lights.

Our ship dropped anchor about 3 A.M., July 5, 1975. We, nine thousand people, gathered on deck, confused at first. Then, one by one, we climbed down the rope ladder. One man led his son by the hand, another carried his old father; one carried his briefcase, another wrapped his property in a blanket and another loosely held a water container in his hand. One was really naked, wearing only underwear. These poor people were warmly received. Not only were U.S. military officers waiting at the port, there were also Red Cross workers, local authorities and some church leaders.

I watched the beginning of the exodus into the foreign land from the deck of the American Challenger. The refugees proceeded slowly into the well-dressed crowd. Everyone, whether Christian or not, was deeply moved by the presence of an old bishop on the deck in the early morning hours.

My fellow countrymen passed by the important persons

cautiously. Carrying sleeping mats and blankets, fathers and sons walked together quietly for nearly fifty feet and then they caught sight of the signs to . . . the showers! Yes, there were the Showers.

The first showers we saw in America stood there in open air. So from the deck I watched people, old and young, quickly undress, rub off the dirt and splash under the showers. Taking a bath so hurriedly at that hour, close to such a solemn setting! I felt lost. "Yes, even in this country, sanitary measures went along with the warmest feelings. Good."

In my country, there is an expression, "rubbing off the dirt". In honor of a friend or relative who just returned from a trip, we might have a party or a dinner "to rub the dirt off from the long journey". The word "dirt" is, of course, used figuratively. And so, I compared the rubbing-off-the-dirt feast in my country with the way people rub off the dirt with soap and water here and could not help but worry for the vast differences between the two cultures.

During our stay in tents on Orote Points, the baths at those open air showers became an important part of our daily activities. From early morning until late afternoon, in the hot sun, people lined up to get to the showers. The gatherings around the showers were quite interesting. With 5, 6 or 7 persons in a small wooden room,—four rooms standing next to each other—, we could look at the sky above, watch the slowly drifting clouds and make conversation with new friends. We discussed many things: the ceremony of lowering the Vietnamese flag on a warship before entering the Subic Bay; the flavor of the ham we'd just eaten; the last days of the nation; getting milk for the babies, etc. Valuable experiences were exchanged, unexpected stories of the fates of friends and relatives were shared under the showers at Orote Points.

In contrast, we had another kind of bathroom at the Fort

Indiantown Gap, Pennsylvania, refugee camp. There, each section had about 100 people with only a small shower, a pitch dark, stifling shower with no window. There was no door either; just a curtain. In that small room, there were three showers so that three people of the same sex could take baths at the same time. There was a cardboard hanging on a curtain with one side reading "Men" and the other "Women". To avoid serious mistakes, one has to check and put out the appropriate side before using the shower.

As the shower was airtight, some people used it as a fumigator. If one caught a cold, he came into the room, then turned on the shower and stepped aside to avoid the hot water. The steam would rise, the man would be soaked with perspiration and eventually would feel much better.

The shower was also used for recording. The refugees were very thirsty for musical tapes. Each family tried to get some familiar songs and favorite voices before they left the camp. Some thought of the shower. About midnight, when most of us had fallen asleep, when all the noises had quieted, one could bring two cassette recorders into the showers. Yes, this was the place for tape recording. With a few borrowed tapes, two recorders together, one as a transmitter, the other as a receiver, the country music lover could continue his work until the next morning.

And it was in the bathroom that I had the chance to listen to the confessions of a man in his mid-fifties.

He was an extremely shy, cautious man. Ordinarily, he seldom talked to anyone in an open manner. Nearly all of us had suffered many heart-breaking losses. Everyday, we moaned, talked on and on while the ladies often cried. Being together for a while, we came to understand the circumstances of others pretty soon, at least in a general way: This lady, wife of a colonel, could get out but her husband and sons got stuck in Vietnam; that fellow, student of the School of Agriculture, ran for his life from B. to N.

province, then from N. to Saigon and met a rescue ship there and now his parents won't know what happened to him; or the family of that wealthy businessman hurriedly climbed on an American ship, leaving behind gold and dollars which could be worth millions of piasters; and so on . . .

However, I didn't know exactly what had happened to the family of that old man.

His was a complete family of husband and wife, a daughter and two sons. It was good enough, for who could expect to have brothers and sisters, aunts and uncles to go with? Yet, there was grief and apprehension on the couple's faces. That concern overruled their surroundings and even spoiled the liveliness of their young sons.

I'd wanted to ask him many times. But at the same time I found that it was not an easy thing to do. I wondered if it might be too curious or crude, especially to a man like him. Besides, he didn't need us; he seemed to be trying to avoid our friendliness.

In fact, I had hardly ever met such a shy man. He was as shy as a girl who just reached maturity. He spoke good English, and it was rumored that he'd been an English teacher for many years. At the refugee camp's main office, he was sometimes asked to do translation for other people. On such occasions he was even more bashful. If someone said something, he listened and remained quiet for a while. He would look at us questioningly as though it was too bold to say. And perhaps, for him, everything was too bold. He'd hesitate again until someone reminded, "Please translate it for me". And again, his attitude was the same.

Would it be too daring to ask anything from such a man?

And then, one night about 11 o'clock, I went to the shower. As I stood in front of the curtain, I read the sign: "Men" and could hear the sound of splashing water inside. I asked, "Who's in there? May I come in?"

14

A cheerful voice replied, "Sure. Please come in."

Raising the curtain, I recognized the shy man immediately. He was unusually kind to me.

"Hello! Feel free, please. More people, more fun. Ha, ha."

He was "feeling free" in the shower, indeed. He was naked and covered with soapsuds. Vietnamese laws do not require a person to cover a particular part of his body in front of someone else, but we don't, however, get accustomed to being nude at public baths as the Japanese do. His attitude really encouraged me. I then started "feeling free."

While I was taking off my clothes, my new friend continued to talk, asking question after question: "When did you leave Saigon? Oh, really? April 29? Half a day earlier than us, then. Which street did you live on? H. Street? We had an uncle who lived on that very street. We used to visit them quite frequently . . . Might have passed by your house, who knows? Ha, Ha. When did you come here? Applied for a sponsor yet? Which one? . . ."

I was amazed and delighted. It seemed to me this man was completely different from the one I had known before. From one topic to another, my friend talked and talked in a cheerful mood while rubbing his body. We treated each other like long time old friends. I soon realized that sometimes displaying human bodies eventually led to displaying human hearts. Once getting rid of all the clumsy clothes, of all artificial relationships, suddenly feeling free, man in the shower would no longer be afraid of any daring act.

Finally, he talked about his own trip:

"My father is 93 years old now. My wife and I had thought about it over and over since N. province was lost. Surely it was time to run away, but what about my father? He's too old and weak to bear any hazard we might encounter during evacuation. As for us, we ran for our lives, not for any trip, didn't we? On the other hand, we wouldn't have peace of mind leaving him alone! I have a younger sister who lived in D. province. Since the loss of that province, I haven't heard anything from her; she's dead or alive, or where is she living now? I don't know. Oh yes, I still have a few cousins, a few nephews and nieces, but they all planned to go. It's hard to find someone to take care of him. To tell you the truth, it's been six years that my father has become more and more senile. He's absent minded and sometimes behaves like a child. Poor father. Whenever he thought about his own age, he asked me to buy a coffin for him."

"A coffin?"

"Yes. A coffin. Traditionally, old men asked for a coffin ready at any time. But that usually happened more in rural areas. Who dares to put a coffin in his home if he lives in the city? It would look terrible, especially since our children cannot accept old customs and habits. That's why we had to keep promising him a coffin, a real good one for when he passed away. Yet people said that if anyone died during the evacuation, the body would be thrown into the sea. As you can see, how could we urge him to throw himself in danger?

"Finally, our relatives met to solve the problem. We concluded that it was almost certain that not all of us would be able to get out. Therefore, anyone who stayed would take care of my father. On the other hand, if we could all get out, then friends and neighbors would be asked for help. All the money and valuable things would belong to those who stayed with my father.

"And then, on April 29, with him seated in a big chair in the living room, all of us, one by one, bowed and thanked him, saying goodbye. We knew this would be goodbye forever.

"What the military situation is, what is happening in the country, what his descendants are trying to do, and so on,

16

I'm sure my father is not clear-sighted enough to understand. But, strangely enough, he could feel that something extraordinary, something tragic, was going on. Yes sir, he sat in the chair with tears flowing gently down his cheeks. We tried to comfort him, but he didn't say anything.

"Later, we packed our luggage. We hid all the money and valuables in a wardrobe and locked it up. An ounce of gold was set aside for buying his coffin. Anybody, friend or neighbor, who decides to take care of him, was entitled to all we left. We couldn't put it all in his pockets as it would be too hazardous for him.

"When we had prepared everything, around 8 P.M., he was still sleeping. It was painful to watch him sleep in the bed, his body all curled up like a small child. We hesitated for a while and then walked away. Waking him up at that time would be a heart-breaking thing to do.

"At that time, enemy forces had advanced into some areas of the city, and the situation was critical. We didn't even know if we could make it out."

"A friend of ours organized the evacuation program which would take place at the port of H. The small boat was so overcrowded that many times, I thought we would not survive. After three days of struggling for survival, on May 2 we were rescued by an American ship in the international territorial waters. We knew then we'd escaped death.

"But sir, it was right at that moment that I was shocked. As I was checking my luggage, I put my hand into my pocket and found that in my hurry I had forgotten to leave the key to the wardrobe for him. My God, I put all the money along with gold and jewelry in the wardrobe, then locked it up!

"I remained silent awhile. Then, gradually, various things appeared in my mind: my father's confusion when he woke up, finding himself alone in the empty house; the scene of our relatives and friends coming in, asking for money we had left; questions about the "hidden key" would be raised; the scene of smashing the wardrobe would frighten him. And thieves and robbers might come in and assault or beat him up. What made me so stupid, so absent minded like that . . . hic!"

The man stopped. He was choking on water maybe. I could hear just the sound of running water. Then he continued:

"My friend, since then I have been obsessed by those terrible pictures. From day to day, month to month, I never feel relieved. God has punished us, you see. I'm so stupid. Hic. I brought the key with me. Hic."

The man stopped again. The water stopped running simultaneously. He had finished his shower. His hands were searching for the towel. Having accustomed my eyes to the dark, I could see his shoulders tremble gently. The man wiped the water from his body and the tears from his eyes.

When did he cry? When I thought he had choked on water? But he was dressing hurriedly as though he was trying to run away. As he stretched his hands out to put his shirt on, I saw a key hanging on a string. There, my old friend carried his key where a Christian typically wears a picture of his God.

Remaining alone in the bathroom, I stood motionless for a while. Then I turned off the water, dressed, raised the curtain and left. Most people had gone back to their rooms and were asleep.

It was a quiet night. The moon was bright in a clear sky. I looked at the shiny moon, touching lightly the key in my hand. Yes, I had a key, kept in my pocket, from a situation similar to that of the old man. (In fact, isn't it true that most of the refugees brought a key along? I mean, who did not feel sorry for a certain mistake, a certain shortcoming he had made to his relatives and close friends who were left behind, something he would feel sorry for the rest of his wandering life?)

Later, a few times, I tried to tell my own story to that man, but it was not easy as he had returned to the attitude he had had before, extremely quiet and shy. Sometimes, I thought he avoided me as though he was avoiding the same mistake or seeing a bad moment in his life again.

I didn't have a chance to meet him again in the shower.

A Day to Dispose Of

Võ Phiến
Translated by Vo-Dinh Mai

It was still light for quite a while after he got home in the late afternoon; about one hour. In the pale sky a few swallows would dash here and there over the rooftops.

One day towards the end of winter Tu returned from work feeling quite tired. He lay down and watched the swallows fly up and down the alley. The birds flew vigorously. They were not flying from a need for displacement. They approached suddenly; then, just as abruptly they would dart away. Their movements seemed pointless, merely to demonstrate their skills, to show off unexpected twists and turns. How many were there? Three or four or more? It was difficult to say. They were everywhere, a joyous sight above the alley inhabited mostly by poor people. In the afternoon when everyone was feeling tired and let down at the end of a day, Tu lay there on his back, watching the swallows until the street lights went on.

It began to rain lightly as the shadows grew darker. When Tu finally got up to make his way to the back yard where the water jar was, the rain wet his hair and the handle of the water scoop was soaking wet when he grasped it.

It continued to rain lightly and silently while Tu ate his supper and even after, when he had finished eating and had lain down to read his papers. He had no idea when the rain stopped.

It was late evening; the moon was bright and cool. In the moonlight the lime-covered burial mound was a startling presence in the front of the house, to the left of the entrance. The old tombstone was covered unevenly with moss. In the moonlight the walk looked even more rough and uneven; the walls of the houses were irregular patches of light and dark; a few pieces of clothing still hung on the lines in the backyards; there was a child's tricycle. Not much of a setting in which to contemplate the moon. But all the same, a moonlit night stirred within Tu an expectation, an excitement, an impatience, even, which he could not explain.

He recalled an old poem, an old verse lurking somewhere, long lost in his memory:

"Twenty-four bridges, one moonlit night" . . .

Twenty-four bridges? What could be more seductive than those dark and light areas of the walls in that small alley, than those discarded old tires lying at the end of the walk, whose pieces of clothing on the line? Nothing much, but then?

Tu wanted to stay awake but it was very late. Some time later he woke up. Somewhere a car was snarling like a wild beast. It was trying to move forwards, then backwards, probably having difficulty turning around. Often at night, people would come to the house next door to gamble and now they were leaving. Headlights reached into Tu's room. In the beams he saw that it had begun to rain again, half-heartedly. It was probably a little past curfew time. After the car was gone, the entire alley was quiet again. Not much of the night was left and Tu went back to sleep.

He awoke again. This time four flarebombs shot up at the same time and hung motionless in mid-air somewhere over Tan Cang, the new harbor. Their light even invaded his mosquito net. He noticed with surprise the seams of his net; he even saw the sheet of newspaper he had put on top of it. The four flarebombs burned brightly and vigorously for a moment and then went out. There remained the cool, blue light of the moon. The rain had stopped. There was not much time left.

21

Later he woke again and heard, far away, the lonely popping of a pedicab someone had just gotten started. The curfew was over. There was not much more time now but he needed some more sleep.

Just as he feared, as soon as he had dozed off, he heard the street vendor crying, "HHHOOOOTTT BBRREAD!" That was the end; from now on, time no longer belonged to him.

✳

Dawn broke like an arm raised high, its fist ready to fall. Tu was afraid of dawn. Each morning was a menace. Every morning was the beginning of a hard day. Every day was a day of work. One thing followed another, one minute, one hour followed others, continuously until evening.

"HHHOOOTTT BBRREAD!"

He opened his eyes. Mist was a vague white outside. He heard the heavy low voice of a pigeon. The heavy, low cooing brought the dawn into deeper silence. Tu wanted to stay in bed longer, to listen to the pigeon but it was already six-thirty, already late. There was no more time for him. There was one hour to go through a few morning exercises, wash his face, shave, go to the toilet, eat breakfast, get dressed and then, after a cursory examination of his bicycle, to jump on it and head for the office.

Tu couldn't afford to get up ten minutes too late. The low cooing of the pigeon, reflections on a quiet, grave morning didn't belong to him. The "moonlit night" of the half-remembered poem didn't belong to him.

"Twenty-four bridges"? Where were they? What were they like? The nights of moonlight he thought of them and it made him yearn for something distant, unreachable. Tu imagined himself alone, wandering, drifting about in that far away, unreal place. But the "twenty-four bridges" didn't belong to him either. He imagined those narrow canals where water ran between rows of trees in the gardens of Lai-Thieu or Cho-Giua, and those forests of thorny bamboo in the highlands of central Viet-Nam, and long, moisture-laden clouds carrying innumerable droplets of water, heavy lazy clouds dragging themselves over the mountain pass of Hai-Ban. Tu imagined the countless little crooks and crannies of the city crawling with life, a busy life full of the unexpected, the life of a hard-pressed people. He imagined the small Chinese coffee shops, the public squares and gardens of Saigon and Cholon, those places where he could sit around and kill time. But those places didn't belong to him. Tu couldn't choose to be there or anywhere else. There was only one place for him to be and that was at the office.

Dawn had arrived like an arm raised high, about to strike and he bent his head, ready to receive its blow.

*

Tu bent his head that morning as he had bent his head the morning before. He had been doing that day after day, year after year. Not one day belonged to him, just for him to dispose of. Making a living was robbing him of his life.

If he decided to go ahead and interrupt the chain of days, to free himself so that he would have the time to do what he enjoyed doing most, to live according to a schedule he arranged himself, then he would be out of work in a few days and in trouble. He did not have the power to stop the flow of things. Looking ahead, far into the future, he could not see the time when a day would come that was his to use and to spend, that belonged to him. On the letters and papers which passed between offices and agencies there was often the phrase, "for your office to take appropriate action." But for him, in the days past and in the days ahead, there never had been and never would be a time to "take appropriate action." A life did not exist in which he could "take appropriate action."

Tu imagined what it would be like. He would stay and watch the renovated folk theater until he was satiated around midnight; then he would walk over to Cho Cu, the old market, to down a bowl of fish soup at one in the morning; then he'd go home to read a couple of chapters of an old Chinese novel. After that he would bring out his stringed instrument and play away, his favorite pieces, over and over, until two or three. Only after that would he go to bed. It would be hardly dawn yet when the Cu bird would utter its low, sad cries in the dew-filled garden and he would listen to those sounds, following each one for a long time, thinking of the damp and chilly dew. He would curl up more tightly in the warm shelter of his blanket and if his wife was in the mood, they'd make love slowly, leisurely. Then he would roll over and sleep again. Outside the gentle, early morning sun would dissipate all the dew and warm up the air. It would be past nine when Tu got out of bed. He would check out all those ambulatory sellers of breakfast who filed past his front door but none would have any food left: hot noodles gone! crab and vermicelli gone! rice and pork gone! He would burst out laughing, contented, and rush outside to buy a piece of French bread and an egg. Then he would make himself a cup of coffee . . . Breakfast over at ten-thirty, lunch at three p.m. That would be a day of "taking appropriate action." A hypothetical day. A magnificent day. A magnificent session of love-making at dawn, a magnificent breakfast at nine in the morning. Tu continued to imagine his extraordinary day and his movements in that day to his heart's content; like a fish in water or a bird in the sky he would dart here and there, making rounds and twists; he would turn the usual order upside down, he would destroy the usual rhythm of life. He surrendered to his imagination with passionate abandon. But where was that day? As far as he could see ahead, it was nowhere.

✳

Nowhere in the future could he see that day, but sifting through the past, he knew that probably he had had one, certainly when he was a child and his father was working to support everyone. He had had those days when he could do whatever he wanted to. In those days his father had been much like Tu was now, trying to take each day as it came. His father had struggled until the last day when he no longer had enough strength left; he had staggered, shuddered like a boat about to sink; he became still at exactly four one afternoon. What a pity! The sun was already tilting in the sky. If only he had lasted two more hours he would have seen the evening swallows flying all over the neighborhood and he would have felt contented and at peace, like a horse that has reached its stall.

Then Tu had begun working. No, it wasn't then that he no longer had free days. He remembered those nights drinking with friends until two in the morning. Then there was that day his colleague, Hung, got married and he was, for some reason, so despondent he walked the streets all night. And that time he was learning to play the flute! He would wait every night until after eleven to climb up to the upstairs porch and blow into his bamboo flute until one or two. There were weekends when he brought his girlfriend to the Cape and returned directly to his office at eight the Monday afterwards. And then there were days when he seemed to be permanently fixed in dark movie theaters with one or another of his girlfriends.

Looking back, Tu was bewildered. One day had followed

another. Every day was a day of work—during that entire time he had worked for a living; yet, when he was younger, he had been able to discover a gap in that continual flow of work, a small gap here or there where he could play the flute and court his girl. It was remarkable.

But then, those gaps became rarer and rarer, harder and harder to find.

One day, during one of those gaps, Tu had met a nice girl. She gave him her address, one of those alleys in Khanh-Hoi. He noted it carefully. When they met again she borrowed a book from him. He was all set later, under the pretext of getting his book back, to come to her house. He had never gotten around with it. Then someone told him she was in love with a young sergeant. How much in love he didn't know and couldn't imagine. But since she was seeing someone else, he left her alone. Some time later he met her again and found she had changed. There was a sadness, a far-away look about her. Yet she was as friendly towards him as before. They became closer and began to meet daily. He learned then that the young sergeant had lost his leg during a military operation. Naturally he wanted to know what was going on between them, if they had any plans. But he couldn't very well ask her, and any comments she made were vague, enigmatic, "It's rough you know." He thought she meant that she didn't have the heart to leave him, yet she was no longer in love. It seemed to him she felt sluggish about the whole thing, or even nonchalant, almost indifferent. He thought that was another aspect of pain and his heart went out to her.

One rather chilly day they lay under a sheet together. She had her arms wrapped around her head, over the pillow. When he looked at her she made a motion as if to unclasp her arms and bring them down. He gently pressed down her arms, keeping them around her head. She resisted weakly, then smiled and gave in. She closed her eyes. While he moved she kept them closed, her face calm. Then she took his lower lip into hers and sucked on it, softly, with concentration, like a child. Tu felt at peace. He didn't rush, didn't wolf it down. He was gentle and slow and deliberate. She went on sucking on his lip, the same soft and slow way. After awhile he stopped moving and looked down and saw that her eyes had opened just a tiny crack. Within that tiny opening her irises shifted back and forth, gleaming. He felt she was insecure and suspicious, prey to some dark disarray. But he went on and she shut her eyes tightly, yielding completely. They were silent all the time. Once in a while he paused, catching again that glimmer of insecurity, of something near panic in that barely perceptible opening between her lids, but he went on again with his love-making.

When it was over, they lay quietly next to one another. The room was in semi-darkness. The air was chilly and time seemed to stretch infinitely. Once in a while Tu was aware of some thought, lonely and listless, like a fly weakly tracing a curve through the space of a quiet afternoon. He remembered that he had come on his friend's body and that thought filled him suddenly with an immense tenderness, a deep and infinite love for her. Her nonchalance, her indifference, summoned their counterparts hiding within him. Unexpectedly then, Tu had come face to face with his growing weariness. The days ahead of him were threatening. He feared them. He felt that from now on he was going to have trouble finding those cracks, those gaps in time when he could enjoy a moment of pleasure, of quiet next to his friend. He did not want to ever part from her.

Not long afterwards, Tu asked the girl and they were married.

✳

Then, as he had expected, the days came and went and he could no longer find one of those moments of leisure.

The time came when he could not even imagine or conceive of finding such a moment. Just fending off the rush of one single morning was enough to leave him exhausted. One day would pass, and as Tu caught his breath, another day was there again.

Now, from its hiding place somewhere on the horizon, the morning sun sprang out and flared against his door, shouting, "Here's another day!" And Tu acquiesced: "Yes." He was unhappy, he complained, but he could do nothing except follow and obey and answer, "Yes."

From now on, until the end of his life, until the last moment of the human race, throughout that long, long stretch of time, the shouts would go on one after another: Another day here! Another day! Another here! Another! Again! Again! The screams and their devilish echoes reverberated, bursting eardrums, hammering into brains, the sounds of fright and hopelessness.

At a certain age, one could still drag one's feet and stop here or there just for a fleeting moment of rest and joy. But one could not rest for long and in the end one capitulated.

✳

In the late afternoon, at the end of winter, Tu came home from work, lay down and watched the swallows darting here and there in the sky above his neighborhood; he worried that night would come too soon, and soon disappear again.

He watched until the swallows had flown away, unaware that rain had begun to fall lightly in the darkness. The rain was falling soundlessly, but after awhile enough water had collected to pour down his roof in thin strands.

Across the alley, over on the porch of Mr. Hai's house, a girl in a white dress was playing with the rain which dripped down from the thatched roof. She probably thought that in the deepening twilight no one saw her or would pay attention to her. She stretched her hand out under the thin strand of water; she teased each drop as it hung at the end of a piece of thatch. She was smiling to herself. Tu understood. A girl of that age was not really playing with the rain dripping from the roof. In reality she was smiling at some joy bursting inside her. She had come out where she thought no one could see her so that, all alone, she could contemplate this delicious turmoil. She teased the drops of water as if she was playing with a puppy or a kitten, while her mind was elsewhere, absorbed with some distant image, some secret yearning.

Tu thought of when he had been going with his wife. How much in love had she been with that young sergeant? Had she ever been like the girl across the alley? He was still bothered by what he did not know. How had she loved the sergeant? All he knew about her was her attitude towards him. He remembered how she had closed her eyes so that he could not see her. Each had his own torment, his own world and there was no trespassing. There was acceptance but it was of a passive kind, made of pain and sadness.

But even all that was far away now. He would never again find those gaps in time when he could watch a woman close her eyes, or when he could play his flute in the middle of the night, or listen to the Cu bird at dawn, or breakfast in mid-morning.

The girl over at the thatched house could still get away with that. "Keep at it," he thought. "Go on, play with the rain drops, yes, go on, and tomorrow, before or after your eight hours of work, try to save a few hours so that.....yes, keep at it."

The rain had stopped. The moon shone over the burial mound, hiding half of the girl's legs. Tu had to think about getting a night's sleep now so he would be prepared and

29

ready for the arrival of the dawn. If not, he would not have enough energy left in his body, and he would not be able to make it through another day, just as, finally, his father hadn't made it.

The young girl could stay up. He wished her all the world.

Requiem

Marguerite Guzman Bouvard
for the Mhung people

With the slow cadence of branches,
the headman lifts his reedpipe.
As he bows, years unfurl
in the throats of grandfathers,

the gait of women in bright plumage,
measuring the seasons,
note by note, a long trek
across China from a land

of mountains and sparse light.
He dances and the forest
contains its mysteries.
His highland, his village

with its rice fields
is the cloth, the clan a thread.
Across the ocean
in a windowless room

men are tapping their pencils,
while their proxy hunts,
his plane dropping bags
of poisoned rice.

From the cockpit he sees nothing.
Only the blur of motors,
the miniature dials of the panel.
He could be crop dusting

in Kansas, one more turn then home
as his country's flag
keeps vanishing, and he
the sorcerer waves his quartz clock

over centuries, green fields.
In the villages, faces
peel like bark. Even the trees
shrink back into their roots.

Karel

Marguerite Guzman Bouvard

In the city you miss the trees.
In New Hampshire with only the birches,
you miss the traffic.

The shadows under your eyes
are dark wells. You carry them
from city to city, on tour

with your guitar. Sometimes your face
is all shadow. You remember
campaigns against *bourgeois decadence*,

the banning of songs, and in '69,
the flight from Prague. In Munich
you have a room, an address.

Home is Kromeriz,
but the borders move;
the language of your brothers changes.

Moravia lives in the peasant's
song, *God who gives us
hunger, give us also bread.*

Landscape of my young world!

Denis Brutus

Landscape of my young world!
Land of soft hills and huts
of aloes and gray-green dreaming firs;
these are the images to lacerate,
against which I glass myself in distance
or a rebellious walling of reserve.
Heartbreaking hillsides and green slopes!
There is no armour to exclude your poignancy,
no blunting, and for me no ease.

I am the exile

Denis Brutus

I am the exile
am the wanderer
the troubadour
(whatever they say)

gentle I am, and calm
and with abstracted pace
absorbed in planning,
courteous to servility
but wailings fill the chambers of my heart
and in my head
behind my quiet eyes
I hear the cries and sirens.

Paris — Algiers

Denis Brutus

I am alien in Africa and everywhere:

in Europe, outside Europe I stand and assess them
—find French racial arrogance and Teuton
      superiority, mouldering English humbug:

and in Africa one finds
chafing, through bumbling,
at the restraints of restraint,
brushing impatiently through varied cultures
in fruitless search of depths:
only in myself occasionally, am I familiar.

New York

Off to Philadelphia in the morning
after blueberry pancakes U.S.A.
with silver images of people
wrestling the racial problem
flickering on my retina-screen;

outside the shark limousines glide
past neons, glass and chrome,
on 42nd nudies writhe
their sterile unproductive lust;

off to Philadelphia in the morning
to rehearse some moulded and half-singing words,
remouth some banal platitudes
and launch-lodge some arrows
from a transient unambitious hand,
a nerveless unassertive gripe.

Ought we to walk on the bruised grass

Denis Brutus

Ought we to walk on the bruised grass
patient, most patient, in the searing cold
grimly — sere yellow, burnt dun — enduring
the winter's weight, its uniform load?

Ought we to add our personal inflictions
—while men lie on concrete
or fumble stones with torn hands
or sigh their cold breath
in the cold unlighted night?

Crossing the Alps: London — Rome

Denis Brutus

Blue pools of peace
high-basined in the snow-flung alps —
beyond the cold, sharp and stony ridges,
the stony shouldered ridges:

another day,
another milestone-journey, milestone day,
a sense of expiring years,
of fated cycles, expired chances and lost grace:

and a dogged thrusting-on
to new places, new names and new marks:
so we carve structure,
so we leave striations in the rocks.

He and He

Ali Morad Fadaie-Nia

Visitor was thinking, Guard was changing his clothes.

Guard said, Your I.D.,

Visitor said, I didn't bring it, I forgot, but I have my photo,

Guard said, Who do you want to see?

Visitor said, An ordinary person, he pays almost five hundred dollars a month,

Guard said, Some pay five hundred, those who have a single, which one?

Visitor said, I forget,

Guard said, What do you mean?

Visitor said, It's on the tip of my tongue, you know, but I forget,

Guard said, You can't find it then,

Visitor said, How many singles do you have?

Guard said, Not a lot,

Visitor said, Well, can I see the list, I might remember the name,

Guard said, The list is in the book here, take a look,

Visitor looked at random, Guard watched the street: From the snow drift on the curb, the stone sidewalk was shivering.

Visitor, talking to Guard to make him busy: Smoke?

No, thanks,

Chocolates?

No, thanks,

Guard, ignoring Visitor, watching the stone sidewalk that has no cover.

Visitor, disappointed, closed the book,

Guard said, If it's important, you can walk up, you've been here before?

Visitor said: Maybe, but I forget,

Guard said, Leave your photo here and go up,

Visitor searched his pockets, found photo, gave it to Guard. Guard looked at it, it was familiar, but more in doubt than certain.

Visitor was not tired, but he came back, he forgot the way out, one of the tenants- very familiar to Visitor- showed him.

As before, Guard was preoccupied with the piece of the stone that was becoming warm from the sun, all his concentration was there.

Visitor said, I didn't find it,

Guard said, What did you want to find?

Visitor said, The room,

Guard said, What room?

Visitor said, I was here before, don't you remember?

Guard said, No, I don't, It's my duty to care about this entrance, this place, understand?

Visitor said, Do you remember my photo?

Guard said, What photo?

Visitor said, When I went upstairs. . . .

Guard said No, I don't,

The sun was finding more of the stone, the piece of stone grows bigger and bigger, branching out, all whitish,

Guard was concentrating on the sun and the stone, not on the coldness: The snow would leave definitely, and stay in the shadow only,

Visitor said, I need my photo,

Guard said, I don't need your photo, If it was here, I certainly would give it back to you,

Visitor said, That is impossible,

41

Guard said, What is impossible? I have only one wallet, you can look yourself. But I'm sure, I didn't take any photo from anyone today,

Visitor said, I really need my photo, this photo is very important to me,

Guard said, Look, as I said before, you can search my wallet, all of it,

Visitor searched: Some papers, no, some money, no, I.D., with photo on it. He looked at the photo: wore a uniform, like the people who have jobs and they wear their job's clothes with a hat even, the face was familiar: eyebrows, chin, even eye-lids and forehead. But Visitor could not remember where he saw it before, he had forgotten,

Guard was not concerned with the sun and the stone anymore: The oldness of the sunset seems like the curtain on the snow and on the stone, covered all. Guard looks like he did not like to watch it anymore.

Visitor looked at Guard, he saw him watching his hand seriously,

Visitor said, Your wallet,

Guard said, What wallet?

Visitor said, Your wallet with your I.D.,

Guard said, I don't remember I gave you anything,

Visitor believed him.

The New One was searching his head with his hand, it was cold and he needed his hat, but he forgot to bring his hat,

Guard said, My shift is over,

Visitor said, Mine is over also,

The sudden wind became a storm, full of used and unused papers, full of I.D's., full of walls, doors. . . .

Visitor was thinking, Guard was changing his clothes,

Eve

Ali Morad Fadaie-Nia

And Adam called his wife's name Eve;
because she was the mother of all living.
Genesis 3.20.

Eventually, she said: "Coffee, just coffee." She played with her cigarettes and looked nowhere. Then, she looked at the window: empty street. The yawn came almost to her face, but it did not happen.

She (the waitress) brought the coffee very soon. She said: "Thanks," to the waitress, and "Well," to herself: "It is hot and a good one, have patience, it will be okay, I mean it is okay now too."

She searched her pocket, found it, took one and lit it up and smoked. She put her elbow on the desk, looked at the waitress. The waitress said: "Something else?" She said: "It's enough, I mean, one more coffee." And smiled, she smiled back. The waitress looked her up and down: She is something, for, put it this way, she (the waitress) loved it.

Two coffees, strong coffees were enough, probably. She saw a paper on a nearby desk, picked it up: "WE ARE LOOKING FOR THE VICTIM, AT LEAST THE DI-VORCE PROBLEM IS SOLVED, THE HOUSE MADE A SECRET MEETING FOR WAR" and "HAMLET, AN OLD FACE," nothing new as usual, she thought. She put the paper back on the same desk. "Anything else?" She (the waitress) said. "No, thanks," she said. She looked at the street through the old window: The rain was coming, but the street was not clean yet, the street seemed as though it could not be clean in any condition. The gray buildings

43

were old like this window, completely quiet somehow. She did not know the place when she came to the street, this coffee shop was the first one she saw: It was twelve o'clock high noon.

*

Very good, this braided hair, artificially, because of her green eyes her manager told her, this, this braided hair, today black, well, it is worth it, green eyes, black hair. Simple clothes, old and beautiful. The job was easy probably, one wink, one smile, change the figure occasionally, there, in the window glass. In the meantime, she thought, it is the time for the next one to come in, but she could not leave, the window glass: Some customers were there watching her, watching the clothes that she wore. She had to stay, till the light is on into the window glass, she must stay there. When the light changes color it means she can leave the stage and go for a rest: Smoking cigarette, drinking coffee. She was tired. She told herself, it is better to stay like a statue, some kind that they used to put in the window glass God knows how long ago. But, she could not do that, the manager told her before, everything has to be natural in the window glass, purely natural. But she stayed like the statue, she could not help it: Head up, tall, black hair down, covering the right breast; covered by the water-lily crepe, simple, flowery. The customer who was watching became angry: Why do they put the statue in the display glass? She heard that and smiled at the customers, it did not work, she showed her naked leg: An eighteen-year-old leg has the aura of some unknown mountain and woman, in the window glass, beautiful and all glass. It worked, that made the customers satisfied. By the way, the light was changed. The other one came in and she left the stage: No smile, no mountain's legs, naked.

She came to the manager, and as usual said: "Can I have a coffee?" The manager said: "Sure." She drank hers back stage, and counted her money: Just for coffee (strong, black, seven per day), food (anything she can put in her stomach), and clothes (pants and a shirt for summer time, and an umbrella for winter, she did not need a coat, not because of the weather—which was cold in winter, dry and cold—no she did not need a coat), and that was all, it was enough, no, it was more than enough. She looked at her breast: Not young any more, but eighteen years of age. She did not know why, did not care why she was remembering her breast's age. The manager said: "Honey again you had a date with the boys." She said: "Yeah." Without care, she said. She did not remember how was that. She did not remember who she was with, even she forgot where was the place she was sleeping last night; actually from dawn to the noon almost high noon. When she came back to the window glass, she was almost naked: The purple shawl came from her neck like a snake on her amber skin, came down on her breasts, which were up, yet young though, then it (the shawl) like a snake-river with the north waves on the navel, knee, playing by the colors: purple, rose, gold, down the navel black and the black, on the labyrinth thousands wings, old very old and blind all blind, but the river comes down and disappears on the middle of the mountain's legs. The shawl was for sale, just the shawl, others free, all.

The time twelve, all black.

East or west, north or south, she was standing on a four way intersection. The hair was not black, the eyes were not green. The shawl was lost. She was standing there. Her eyes were everywhere and nowhere. She was there and she was not there. She wanted to lean on the street's light, but she could not. She seemed she is waiting, she did not look waiting. She crossed the street when the light was green. The other side, she stayed again, searched for the cigarette, it was empty, she came back to the west side of the street again. She came to the east, north. Now, it was—the street—quiet, empty. She did not know the place, it was the first time she was coming to this four-way intersection. She did not remember how she came here. She looked at the people who were coming up or going by. She looked and she did not look. She just knew one thing for sure: It will be over, somehow. She did not know how. She did not care how. Her skin needs something probably. She looked and saw the water-lily was trembling in that shop across the street. Male or female? It does not make any difference, as it was someone, it was enough, or it was not enough, it does not make any difference, to her, either. She looked at one.[1] It was better than staying at the four way intersection, she thought. She gestured to one, who was coming toward her with the smile, as usual, there was dawn, four o'clock, eventually.

In Farsi (Persian language) used as a pronoun for the third person singular, male and female both.

From Q to all the future

Ali Morad Fadaie-Nia

The first one, who seemed to know me for a long time, said: You'll not walk there, certainly. Without waiting for my answer, he put my right leg on the shelf and said: It's mine.

The second one, walking into my house, looked as though she were my roommate, and she collected all the furniture I had gathered. She talked to herself continuously: "No, he doesn't need this one, doesn't need that one. . . ." She put them in her bag. She did not even look at me. "This? It makes a problem for him." Even everything on the verandah was taken; this piece of flower, even, that black and white photo—which was of myself in the future or years past—even my nostalgia pen which was only used to pay bills lately, doing nothing else, this pen, I mean, on my desk—even one or two family pictures on my desk— no identity, whose family I did not know, not knowing anyone in the photograph, but whom I identified as my family, even. Sometimes she stopped to see what the others might do. Then she got busy collecting everything and put them all in her bag.

Another one said, No, you don't need these clothes. He took the shirt off my back.

Still another one said, The hands, the hands need an extra place; you don't need them over there. He took out my shoulder blades, the forearms, fingers.

I was surprised that no blood spurted out from my body, but I was engaged by this cutting without redness, and I imagined: It would be a red frame, fresh, young, with black and white on it, and it at least could be a memory.

47

My body seemed to have no bones, or if it had, they were out of date goods, ones which no one would buy, even, nobody would want them for free, either.

The bag lady seemed to want to wash her hands, and she put them in my breast—left side from my view, right side from hers—and looked away at something I did not even see at all and then somehow looked at me: Take care of yourself and don't keep this junky stuff in your house.

The person who was interested in legs—without showing any favor to me—said goodbye quite friendly-like, but not to me, rather to the bag lady.

The person who liked my hands talked to one who came for my eyes: Yes, you can have it. Eyes? No, he doesn't need them, they are only a weight for him. This guy, without looking at me, seemed to be putting a spoon in a tea cup or taking an olive from a plate with his fingers, and he took away my eyes.

I loved and admired the way they worked. None bothered any other; they were relaxed, they did their jobs perfectly.

Some place in my vertebrae was changed. I thought, I can see it in the mirror that is hung on the wall or, no, it was a part of the wall. I went toward the mirror, I didn't see anything, anybody, only some dark knot from this side, moving to that side, into itself, all these times, as usual.

You

Ali Morad Fadaie-Nia

In the train station I saw this man, maybe twenty years old, with a black and white beard, selling black and white flowers or giving them to the people free.

Why give them away free? I asked.

He said: Because it is propaganda for my beard.

I said: So well. . . . Which is usually what I say when I do not understand what it means.

But he understood and asked me: Where are you from? I said: Bibian.

Then he said: They sell black and white rings there.

I said: For propaganda, also-

He said: No, they collect the money to throw you out of there, you . . .

They don't give them free, too? I asked.

No, they die free there, he said.

What do you mean by that?

He said, You know what I mean, you, especially you, coming into our streets, you plant rings, grow cactus, you're a magician, you don't even recognize me now. But your picture is with me, along with your wife and your five-six year old daughter who still looks like she's seven, after all these years. . . .

I said, You can't be serious young man, sell your flowers. The train leaves in a few minutes.

But he insists on his words and he holds me there, searching his pockets and taking out a black and white photograph: I am there old, close to the portico of the ring seller's shop, my daughter—she mostly looks like her

49

mother—has long black hair, her face afflicted by April, it's so fresh.

You don't believe it, do you? he asked.

The picture is okay, I said, but I am only thirty years old.

So you're making magic again, he asked, and then changed the subject: it's like smuggling to sell flowers here. But wait I'll be back soon.

It was my wife, who loves to wear uniforms, like a policeman, like a soldier—she scared him.

My wife asked, What were you doing? The train leaves in a few minutes. Hurry up. . . .

When she makes a command, as usual, I have no choice. She took my hand and dragged me toward the train.

I looked out a window of the train: between the old buildings, around the new cemetery, I saw the black and white bearded fellow, holding my daughter's hand, dragging her toward the train station. Without looking at her long hair, I saw her eyes were all one, all one the freshness of April.

This woman close to me, this delicate lovely wife, in her usual way said: It's bad luck to look at the cemetery. What are you looking for?

And I, just to say something, said: In the train station. . . .

One Minute of Salt

Armando Valladares
Translated by Marguerite Guzman Bouvard

To the thousands of men,
women and children who drowned
in the sea while trying to flee communism

One minute of salt for the silence
                    of those who could not
return to dust.
Jehovah surely forgot the waters,
those who died
among the murmuring waves,
their mouths brimming with algae,
their eyes devoured by fish,
those who were anchors of rotten
                         flesh,
modern Jonahs dismembered
in the bowels of sharks.
One minute of salt for the silence
of those who disappear
without name or memory,
those who sank
when they were searching for light
and the word,
those who were raked by bullets
while dreaming of liberty in their rafts,
those who have no stones,
no crosses,
who lie I don't know where
because there are no tombs in the waves.

September Song

Armando Valladares

Translated by Marguerite Guzman Bouvard

To my wife who is always near

Singing to you
today my words have
a sad echo
the deepest echo perhaps
of my mountains
gentle
far away
insistent
amplified by time-scarred days.
Through the old and loving prison bars
          —of our common prison—
the gray shell of dawn opens
like the rain insistent now
from the very sky that was beginning.
With each breath I take
through the broken ribs
of those barbed wires
your memory grows within my hands
breaking the locks
that seal morning.
Because I sing to your silence
my tortured poems
become tenderness.
Because I sing to your presence,
today I am more than ever a free man
and I waken to hope with September.

September 5, 1981

Free.....?

Armando Valladares
Translated by Marguerite Guzman Bouvard

To all those in Cuba who wear shirts
with lettering across their chests saying,
"I am a free man."

You say you are free
—I don't know whether you believe it
but at least you say it—
Freedom is not the space
to take a few steps,
or a bed
for lying down by twos.
You say you are free
but you have no words
because you only repeat
the words they give you
—with your mouth closed—
Freedom is not bread
—sometimes on the table—
nor some beer
or something to smoke.
Freedom means to do this:
to write what you think,
to cry out at what you detest
even though you may pay for your poems
with years of torture,
even though you may die of imprisonment
in this isolation.

But It's Only A Feeling

Armando Valladares
Translated by Marguerite Guzman Bouvard

Now I have no nights.
All my time is daytime,
an artificial day
of burning bulbs.
I sense that outside
there are whispering stars
and clouds
and a moon
that sails among them
but it is only a feeling.

It has been raining blindly
since twilight.
Even from far away
I hear its ringing
repeat the spell
—or rather the melody—
as it falls and falls.

Gunfire shatters
the quiet dawn.
A siren wakes up
and dogs bay.

54

Then, in the distance
the voices of the guards.
A rat-tat-tat,
and a longer volley,
and again, silence.
I sense that there is a dead man
at the foot of the barbed wire
but it is only a feeling.

I know that a cyclone is approaching
—even though no one told me—
This is October
and outside the wind is blowing
with increasing force.
It can be heard on the other floors,
hammering the windows.
But where I am
the wind will not come in.
My windows
are nailed shut the year round.

It is already spring
but not in this room.
The sky must be blue
and embroidered with birds.
The wind must be stirring
with a freshness in its breath.
I sense that the fields
are a deep green
and studded with flowers
but it is only a feeling.

Faithfulness

Armando Valladares
Translated by Marguerite Guzman Bouvard

You have waited so long
with your constant love
—ever since you believed in the miracle
of the wounded rocks—
when you learned to cry inside
over things nobody could understand
—or almost nobody—
You waited
because hope is something
that cannot be taught
like the catechism of hate
like the anguish of expectation.
Only you
have been at the end of the road
with your arms opened
in a cross of tenderness
—like the one you wear on your breast—
with the self-denial
you carry in your soul
until my return
for which you have waited all these years.

They Have Not Been Able

Armando Valladares
Translated by Marguerite Guzman Bouvard

They have not been able to take away
the rain's song
not yet
not even in this cell
but perhaps they'll do it tomorrow
that's why I want to enjoy it now,
to listen to the drops
drumming against
the boarded windows.
And suddenly it comes
through I don't know what crack
through I don't know what opening
that pungent odor
of wet earth
and I inhale deeply
filling myself to the brim
because perhaps they will also
prohibit that tomorrow.

The Best Ink

Armando Valladares
Translated by Marguerite Guzman Bouvard

To Rene Diaz Almeida, poet and brother in the struggle.

They have taken everything from me
pens
pencils
ink
because they don't want me
to write, and they have lowered me
into this torture cell
but not even with this can they drown my defiance.
They have taken everything from me
—well almost—
because I still have my smile,
the pride of feeling myself a free man
and in my soul a garden
of perennial flowers.
They have taken everything from me
pens
pencils
but I still have the ink of life
—my own blood—
and with it, I still write poetry.

original written with my blood and a wooden
splinter in April, 1981 in the torture cells of
Combinado del Este prison in Havana.

And My Prison Bars Bloom

Armando Valladares
Translated by Marguerite Guzman Bouvard

To my unforgettable wife

Today it has been fifteen years
that they surrounded me with barbed wires,
bayonets and locks,
that they forbade me
time and space
light
sun
air.
For fifteen years
blows and kicks
have memorized my body
and the maddening escalation
of psychological torture
rocks each cell
in my brain.
Today
in the darkest corner
of my fifteen year isolation
I close my eyes
and then I have the sun
and happiness and love
and my prison bars bloom tenderness
because I have you.

When We Meet Again

Armando Valladares
Translated by Marguerite Guzman Bouvard

I shall return
in spite of the hateful silence,
in spite of the rain and the abyss.
Then, they will not matter,
the horizon of bayonets
at my back,
the barbed wire hills
that bristle
as if they suspected
the joy of our meeting.
The gods have planned this
and an inexorable destiny
will open the gates and paths
for my love
for our love.
It will happen
in the name of all beliefs
with the fervor of all our hopes
for a new dawn,
not like the ones we wakened to
a thousand times
with empty eyes.
I shall come to you
without fail this time.
Our meeting has already been decided
despite the hate and the abyss.

Exile

Rose Moss

Stephen Katela dozed at the back of the car. Occasionally he opened his eyes to look at the two dark heads in front of him, the kind white couple who were taking him to their home. Yesterday he had been at another college and had given a talk on African music, and another kind white couple had taken him home as their guest, and he had talked about South Africa. He closed his eyes. A theme kept palpitating under the surface of his attention, its outline blurred like a cat in a bag, like his own young body when he crept down to the bottom of his mother's bed and thought that no one could see him because it was dark under the blanket. His brother played with him there, a touch and move game in the shapeless dark, a hiding-go-seek without rules, until they started to wrestle and wriggled so fast they rolled off the bed onto the humorless floor. Then their mother scolded them while she fed another baby mielie pap with one hand and attended to the tea and remaining mielie pap on the stove with the other. Stephen and his brother went out to play until she called them in to breakfast. They ignored her injunctions to take soap and wash under the tap in the yard. Winter was too cold for washing. She would come out when the baby was fed and give them a slap and another scolding, would oversee their mutual lathering and squirming at the tap, and when the relics of their brief exploration had been washed off them— cinders of a brazier in which they had poked for coal, gritty smears if they had been examining the rubbish in the street—she would fold them into the bosomy warmth of the room. The reminiscent smell of early morning fires, the

61

grey blue haze of the township, bit like an acrid, toxic gas into the tissue of Stephen's memory. He opened his eyes again to fill them with the two silhouettes in front of him, the white couple driving home through a heavy mist that the headlights held pale and solid, close to the car.

The road twisted and heaved. They had come off the smooth turnpike, homogeneous from Virginia to Maine, that made Stephen feel that this whole lecture tour was an hallucination in which distance had no more dimension than in a dream. Episodes that repeated the same obsessional pattern followed each other arbitrarily in settings that differed only like the scenery of an impoverished theatrical company. Every road was the same road. The arrangement played with slightly differing signs and overpasses, discreet banks of grass, and trees that only gradually and reluctantly admitted the grey agglomeration of cities whose suburbs had long been suppressed by the same green uniform as the countryside. At last, off the highway, an idiosyncratic thrust from the land molded the road into a pliant index of fields and streams, pulled straight over flats, packed more densely in steep valleys and rises. The mist was so thick he could hardly see the vegetation. From the dancing swell of the road he could imagine himself back on the stretch between Mooi River and Pietermaritzburg where frequent mists nourished the land, and cattle condensed the airy whiteness into substances richly edible— for those who could afford to buy them.

But every now and then a leafy intrusion over the road caught his eye, the uneven bars of a wooden fence, or irregular stone globules of a wall, and Stephen was reminded by these foreign shapes and colors that he was not on that Natal road, he was somewhere in New England, going to spend the night in a strange house among strangers. These sights, like foreign substances grafted among the tissues of what he had seen, lived, and compounded into organic constituents of his own self, set up a resistance. Each reminder that he was not home accelerated an irritation, a process of rejection. His body, his perception, the accumulated chemicals of his own being barred these alien elements and tried to seal their pernicious proximity off from himself, to cast them off like a foreign skin or organ, to expel all toxic strangeness. He shut his eyes. He tried to lull himself. Let him not think that if he did not learn how to assimilate America there would be nothing left for him to see, no place where he could retain that dwindling self he felt to be his own. He thought of his brother and the dusty soccer field where they used to play when their mother went off with the baby and a bundle of washing wrapped in a sheet, to the white city where she worked until night came. How did that theme shape?

His host was also a composer. Stephen had heard a quartet by him. It had been played at one of the colleges where Stephen had contributed to a symposium on modern music. There had been lectures and workshops during the day. In the evening there was a concert and Ken Radley's String Quartet, cited as an example of some of the finest composition in the United States, was played to instruct an audience that might find such compositions hard to come by. To Stephen the quartet seemed unintelligible, thin, and boring, but he blamed his response on his own ignorance. Ken's quartet was one of the many signs, like billboards on the road, that said to Stephen, "We don't speak to you. We are not written in your language. You have nothing to say to us."

The car slowed, turned up a driveway, and they had come. "We're here," Janet announced smiling. This was her home. Stephen smiled to her. They were so kind. Ken opened the door and light flared out of the amber hall over damp steps. Inside there was more light.

"Why don't we wash and have a drink while Janet's preparing supper?" Ken suggested. "I'll show you your room," and he took Stephen's suitcase, which he had already fetched from the car. Stephen wondered whether it was right to let Ken carry his suitcase; or did he feel uncomfortable because Ken was white? "I'll take it." He reached for the handle. Ken let him take it and picked up another suitcase. He led the way up carpeted stairs, pointed out the bathroom, and gestured inside the doorway of a room at the end of the passage, "This is yours. See you downstairs." With a quick smile he indicated his confidence that Stephen could manage from this point. He could, in a manner of speaking. He had done it before. He took the smaller of two towels neatly waiting for him at the foot of the bed, and the cake of soap, still wrapped, and went to the bathroom. It retained the old-fashioned tub of an old house, but a combed sheepskin on the floor and a shelf over the tub for an ashtray, two detective stories and a small vase of brightly dyed star flowers indicated that it was not a room where Ken and Janet expected austere behavior.

When he came back to the room they had given him Stephen noted the artifacts of someone else's life. A childhood unimaginably unlike his own surrounded him. Behind the bed hung a drawing of the beach. The sea was a properly undulating blue on whose conventional waves there sailed the black outline of a yacht, innocent of the relatively immense fish whose profile stood mute, motionless, and symbolic between it and the yellow and purple sand, where a green scribble suggested grass. In a low bookcase under the window, children's books about shells and birds, adventure stories, Webster's illustrated dictionary, a microscope under a plastic cover, indicated another layer of the American boy's life. The most recent stratum was evidenced near the dressing table where a poster of Humphrey Bogart ignored college pennants and the image of the alien in the mirror.

Stephen sat on the bed. He felt his knees under his palms. He insisted on his own undeniable life, on his own childhood in and out of the dusty location and the dusty mission school, on his skill to be as slick as a tsotsi who wore tight trousers and carried knives. He had been as mocking as a mosquito when he played the pennywhistle on street corners, when he demanded a penny, a tickey, a sixpence, baas. He went downstairs for a drink.

Janet was busy in the kitchen that was separated from the dining area and lounge by a wooden counter. He noticed that she was wearing a string of those grey seeds that white women didn't think smart in South Africa. Here they were favored by the wives of college professors, like Janet, and girl students from good homes.

It was fine to sit in the same room as a busy woman preparing food. "Haven't you got some vegetables to peel?" he offered. In America it was all right to help like a piccanin.

"It's all done, frozen and sliced," she laughed, "Very American." She untied her apron and hung it over a rail. "Come and have a drink."

How casually legal it seemed to her to offer him a drink. How legal and unremarkable to be alone with a black man. In South Africa when white women offered him drinks, he was wary. Even at mixed parties he felt his safety as sharp as a blade's edge. With Cynthia Barton he would drink; after dinner, meat and wine, she offered him brandy and liqueur. After slow talk and darkness he would wake to hear his heart slamming, police banging the door, and his brother crying, sick. When the police arrested David Msimang with a white woman and found out that he was a musician, they broke his eardrums, just for fun. After that, Stephen would not visit Cynthia alone any more, and on the phone she said, "For goodness sake, don't *explain*. There's nothing to *explain*. If you don't want to come, don't come. You don't owe me anything. I'm not your white madam." She never allowed him to tell her about David Msimang.

In New York he went to some mixed parties given by Andrew Mohone. South Africans who had left with the cast of *King Kong*, after Sharpeville, after Mandela, after Sobukwe, after waves of arrests under the sabotage laws, after Voster, on scholarships, on exit permits, on passports and family money, met each other at mixed parties and felt that the old risk and thrill could be recaptured. They repeated the gestures of defiance that here did not defy, and knew again that they were singly brave and free. Some of the whites at Andrew's parties were Americans—young reporters, instructors at Columbia and the Free School, churchmen with missionary acquaintances—a miscellaneous lot who, like the South Africans themselves, of different generations and concerns, seemed to have little in common but a geographically named node of feeling. By two o'clock in the morning the parties had usually divided into Siamese twin parties, one black, one white. In South Africa the mixture would have lasted all night. Mixed parties here missed the police.

Once or twice black separatists came instead of whites. They made remarks to Stephen like, "I can see you come from Africa. Your face is so proud." They had never heard his music. The mixed parties were easier. At first, the old South Africans asked him for news and gossip. "Do you know Diana Zindberg? . . . What's she doing now?"

"Didn't she marry an Englishman? I think she married an Oxford don," someone would supply. Or she was "on the West Coast now," or she had remained in South Africa.

A few people knew Cynthia Barton, and asked whether he knew her. "Yes, I think she's still in Johannesburg."

"Goli, hey! Good old Goli! Man, I still miss the place. Well Cynthia was a great gal," as though she had partially died, "Just a great kid! I wish she'd come here."

Why? Stephen wondered, why did anyone wish that?

He imagined that in New York there were such parties given by White Russians, Serbians, Spanish anarchists, Palestinian Arabs, Ghanaians and Czechs. All exiles, all dying. When all his oxygen was exhausted he would also relish thin gossip about South Africa and the people of his generation, become a comfortable exile, a cell in the specific tissue of exiles and cosmopolitans who had by now become organically accepted and integral in the American metabolism.

Ken entered from another room. "There's a letter from Christopher. He says he'll stop by on his way to New York," he told Janet.

"Good. When'll that be?"

"Anytime."

"Christopher's our son," she explained to Stephen. "He's been summering in the Hudson Bay area. He says there are some interesting algae there. Algae are his thing." She smiled fondly, indulgently.

The remoteness of these lives that he saw in midstream pressed in on Stephen. There was none of his own air left, none of the spacious sunlight, naive and simple, by which he had learned to read the world. Here, existence was compounded into individual complex studies and specialized fields. Each man saw his own topic, noted its intricate interrelationships and structures, and guessed at the intricacies known by others. In South Africa he had written music, it seemed to him now, like a child. He had composed as though he could pour sound simply into the heart of another man, a heart unobstructed by perceptions evolved to assimilate incommunicable knowledge. Here his communications were defined. He was a practicing composer, and an authority on the music of Southern Africa. He had become a curiosity devoted to curiosities, the speaker of an arcane language—composer, consequently, to no ear but his own. The longer he stayed the more arcane his music must become; it must breed into itself to retain that exotic worth that was supposed to give it value. It could not mate again with the sounds of his daily life, now American—that would breed an impurity into his sound, a new idiom into his voice. And then he would lose that now ghostly audience in South Africa who, when they listened to his music, thought that the earth sang and the cicadas chorused together, and did not know that their unique earth was quaint veld, their noon remote from others'.

Each of these Americans with his intricate knowledge constituted one cell of this complex society whose function was a life other than Stephen's, whose purpose was something he did not know, and could not, without destroying himself, adopt. If he did not adopt its purpose, America would shake him off as an intrusion, a piece of a foreign body, a cell or organ that lived by the principles of some other body born under the Southern Cross.

Something of Stephen's loneliness emanated through to Janet. It prompted her to the inbred courtesy that required her to turn the topic of conversation to her guest's interests rather than her own. She reserved the subject of Christopher and his letter for later, for that conjugal conversation whose even tenor is like the even conversation a man conducts with the sights and texture of his belongings and his people. She would deal with Christopher in a time and a language from which Stephen felt sealed off as if from the air of life. She asked him questions about South Africa while they sipped gin and tonic with wedges of lime—a drink he had never known in South Africa, even at the mixed parties of Houghton and Northcliff, and certainly never in the shebeens. At last she came to the question that all these polite, interested Americans asked.

"Will you ever go back?"

"I can't. I got out illegally, without a passport. I'm a refugee."

"You mean they wouldn't give you a passport. Why on earth not?"

"They've had some bad experiences with the wrong people getting out and making propaganda against the government overseas. We Africans talk too much."

Ken liked his dryness. "And have you talked too much here?"

"I've been on a lecture tour." They laughed.

"Your topic's not very incendiary," Ken pursued.

"No," Stephen agreed, "But I do some damage in ordinary conversations like this. And then, most Afrikaners, especially those who deal with us, are ignorant. They're afraid of people like me because I'm not a simple Kaffir."

"How did you get out?" Janet wanted to know.

"Oh, there's a sort of underground railroad, and a refugee center in Dar-es-salaam."

"Will you go back there?"

"I don't know what will happen to me." After he had spoken he heard the passive helplessness he had revealed. Ken heard it too.

"Why do you want to go back to South Africa?"

"I don't." But Ken ignored this reply. His waiting silence was as heavily palpable as a waking sensation that presses into sleep and breaks its integuments. And like a sleeper who begins to talk before he has quite shaken off sleep, and talks as truthfully as in a dream, Stephen continued.

"I can't work here. I say to myself that tomorrow, or next week I'll be able to, but I can't. I compose, but it's all false. I can't bear to listen to it. I don't think I can write outside South Africa."

"Then you must go back." Ken spoke the imperative that Stephen feared. He brought into it the auditory reality of an American accent with a resolute inflection that Stephen would never have invented in his own mind, the instruction that, like the ground bass of a passacaglia, had sounded

69

without interruption in Stephen's feelings for weeks. Stephen repeated, "I can't." Ken and Janet said nothing. "If I go back I'll be in prison within a year—not a nice comfortable prison where people can write their memoirs. I'll be in a South African jail where people get beaten up and tortured and go mad. I've been in prison. A pass offender gets kicked around. Sometimes he's sent to work on potato farms where he wears a potato sack, winter and summer. Sometimes he's beaten for not working hard enough. They knocked the eardrums out of a friend of mine because he was a musician. Some people get beaten to death. In the jail they put ten men in one cell, and give you one bucket that gets full long before morning. There are no beds. You sleep on the floor, as far away from the bucket as you can. And I'm not a pass offender. I can't expect such good treatment. I'm not likely to write much music there."

"Then you must learn how to write here."

"How? How can I learn anything like that?" Stephen breathed hard on his rage. These Americans thought they could solve everything. They had no respect for boulder weight, for things too heavy for a man to lift.

"I don't know. I guess it's easier to say than to do. Just give yourself time to hear what this country sounds like. You probably just need time."

"Yes," seconded Janet, "After all, you haven't been here very long."

Their unsuffering sympathy fed Stephen's rage. "I want to write in my own language. In South Africa that isn't allowed. An African has to speak English or Afrikaans, a composer has to learn the sonata form and the instruments of the European orchestra. They are what he must write for. There's an instrument we have in Lesotho—a bow and a string, and a gourd for resonance. It plays two notes. The person who plays it can hardly hear it himself, it's like a whisper, like a lover. In a world that's so quiet, there's room for an instrument like that. There are nothing but mountains, and one bad road. It keeps the cars out. The people are too poor for radios. All they can afford is the sound of a gourd, like the earth, like the sunlight, like being poor, like being black. You can't hear it in Johannesburg—even the Africans are too rich there, or their being poor is a cramping vise. That bow and gourd says what I want—but where could I play something like that in America? No one would hear it. Everything's so loud here, the cars, the radios, the fire trucks, planes. I can't hear anything human, alive. And even if anyone could hear my bow and gourd, what would they make of it? Two simple notes over and over, so monotonous. Not at all . . . psychedelic." He smiled at this disparaged word of praise, as if to overcome squeamishness at having used it. "I sound angry, but I'm not angry at Americans for being what they are. That's what they are. It's incurable. Like being an African. But it's at the other end of the world, and I can't make myself learn what to be again, like a baby. I don't start from nothing. I'm a man already."

Ken and Janet were embarrassed at this outburst. Their habitual withdrawal from involvement with strangers, especially strangers whose insoluble problems could grieve and fester in those whose pity held no power to remedy; an accepted training rooted in the manners of ancestors who knew that what is delicate must be protected (sometimes by deliberate ignorance), who would not mention rape, drunkenness or money in front of women; and a traditional stoicism that would not weep but fastened troubles to the self like a brace to keep men upright—all made them withdraw from Stephen's demand.

Ken spoke first. "I hope you'll take advantage of the musical opportunities in these parts. There'll be some interesting concerts in New York this fall, and other things too. I've got a notice from Hunter College. I'll look for it after supper. You will be in New York, won't you?"

"Yes." Stephen didn't tell him that he received his own notices, invitations, introductions.

"And I've got programs for Lincoln Center. I can often get complimentary tickets . . ."

Stephen saw how the problems of the boy Christopher must have been kindly finessed away until he grew up into, not quite a man—for he was allowed no human, intractable troubles, only those his society could digest—but an expert on algae.

Christopher came home that night. Stephen heard him arrive, and the noise of welcome and explanation that a guest was sleeping in his room. "Then you must go back," Ken had said in an American voice with an unforeseen inflexion. "Then you must go back." The initial staccatos of greeting sank into long blurred sentences, and Stephen tried to fuse the reawakened rhythm of family discourse in his ear with the theme that had struggled forward during the drive through the mist, the song of playing with his brother in the morning. But he could not achieve the fusion, and fell asleep again.

He met Christopher at the breakfast table. Ken introduced him to the bony youth. "Steve's giving a paper on African music at Fenmore Hall this afternoon, and going to New York tomorrow."

"I think I'm in your room," Stephen said tentatively.

"I'm only camping here," Christopher assured him. "I'm going on to New York myself."

"Perhaps Chris can give you a ride down," Ken suggested, "Unless you'd rather fly . . ."

During the meal Christopher accompanied firm gestures that reached for butter or toast on the well-known table with stories about his summer. He talked about what his expedition had accomplished. "We collected hundreds of specimens that are probably new. How'd you like an alga named after you, mother?"

"I'd have to see it first," she joked.

"I've got slides. Are you free tonight? Can we look at them?"

Janet drew him back to arrangements for the day. "I've been waiting all summer for you to help your father clear out the cellar."

"That'll be great," Christopher assented before Ken could protest.

Stephen wondered whether his help would be welcome or obtrusive. No, he'd work on the location theme, even though nothing would come of it.

While he was sitting at the desk the boy Christopher must have used, Stephen saw them walking through the grounds. Sometimes they stopped to examine a change or permanence. The two men walking among trees, their heads flickering among bright foliage, who lived in that world inhabited by squirrels and jays that he had sometimes read about in northern storybooks, were indeed men, not plastic surrogates produced by a society that forbade suffering and wanted only organs of perception, units of intelligence, consumers. These two were men, father and son, archetypal, and as mythical to Stephen as woods that harbored plentiful creatures, as strange as snows and blueberries and maples. Such familial affluence was unknown to him. His father had been one of the men who lived with his mother for a few years and then disappeared into the jails, into the labyrinth of townships around Johannesburg, or into the reserves. A series of men had played with him and the other children, in idle friendliness. Nostalgic for a life some of them had never known, they assessed him as a candidate for initiation, and told him stories to inspire warlike heroism, sagas of Zulu impis led by Chaka and Dingaan. But often they were irritable. The children seemed always underfoot, Sarah wanted more money to buy them clothes, and Stephen was always wasting candles at night when a man wanted darkness and Sarah's hard breathing.

Stephen and his brother knew the world directly, not by

the mediation of fathers. There were not discrete worlds, one filled with talking animals and fairies for children, another with money and taxes and politics for adults. It was all one world. Grown men as frightened as children of policemen who, as irresistible as witchcraft, might bang on the door in the middle of the night to ask for a pass, or dig up the floor to look for skokiaan. It was all one world. In an acid dawn as pink as millions of pounds, neighbors climbed onto bicycles and rode into the city; on the way to the long queue at the bus stop they stepped on the hoar that clung to wisps of dry grass and paper; some who had slept with braziers in closed rooms breathed the warm air too long and did not wake up in time for life. Nothing was omitted except this other world, inconceivable—the house set among wild trees and lavish grass, this world that the father and the son were revisiting, and had never altogether left, and this kind of humanity that grew among them. Stephen could never revisit his childhood. Now he must live in a world that his childhood had never guessed existed.

That night Christopher showed them slides of his expedition to the Hudson Bay. Beyond sight or sound of any other human life small villages grasped tight in dour friendliness. Granite boulders grew lichens like birthmarks, and in their brief summer thronged with silky flowers that looked like Karroo vygies. Pane after pane of light offered visions that Stephen could understand—emptiness, light, virginity—where he had expected only more that was alien, unassimilable. In a landscape like this one could play an instrument with two notes. But he was afraid to think of what he saw. Would he go to the Hudson Bay to try another kind of exile?

Being driven to New York, he asked about the expedition. "Didn't you feel lonely?"

"No. There were seven of us on the ship, and we got to know some of the village people quite well. Strangers are very welcome. And it's not as if there aren't any phones. I called my girl in New York twice a week. It's not half as bad as it'll be next year when we go to Lake Baikal, if we can arrange it. We might go to Antarctica instead. What's Cape Town like? They say it's beautiful."

"I've never been there. The government tries to keep us Africans out of Cape Town."

"Oh, I thought most of the population was negro."

"In Cape Town there are a lot of people of mixed blood. They're called coloureds and are treated differently from us. Every shade of whiteness deserves a special degree of privilege."

"You must be really glad to be out of it."

"I am. Don't you ever get homesick when you go to these strange places?"

"I guess I've never been away long enough. It's no problem really. I could come back any time." They seemed to have come to a dead end. "Do you ever get homesick?"

"Sometimes."

"I guess people get homesick for the strangest things. One of our research team comes from Anatolia. He longs for sheep's eyes. Look for *that* in a supermarket!" Christopher laughed.

Stephen was silent.

"Mind if I turn on the radio?"

"Go ahead."

Sometimes they let the clamor of baroque music substitute for conversation. Sometimes they spoke through it.

"Why did you come to the States? To get out of South Africa?"

"Partly. And people always told me I should go overseas to finish my education. They said my composing needed to be finished." He smiled at the private irony.

"But your family's still there?"

"My mother."

"Have you got brothers, or sisters?"

"Most of them died as babies. One brother grew up with me, but he died when I was in high school."

"Your mother must miss you."

"I don't know. I wrote, but didn't get an answer. And I asked someone I knew to look for her, but I haven't heard from him either."

"Why don't you phone."

"We haven't got phones. In the locations, only white officials have phones."

Vivaldi gave way to Cimarosa by way of a commercial. How must it be to live in Christopher's world, where there was no sensual space, distance, silence, darkness? Stephen remembered reading that a night of darkness had come upon New York like a disaster. How must it be to live like that, deprived of any sense of the given light, and the given earth's autonomous being? How would it be to live in America and lose all stillness, loneliness, man-otherness, to live in a world where the whisper of a string in a gourd could never be heard, imagined? Christopher could hardly be five years younger than himself, but Stephen felt old, old-fashioned, old as chameleon who first allowed the news of death to be brought into the world, old as death, incomprehensible to Christopher. Christopher lived in the new world. Was there any music Stephen could write for him? What was there in Christopher's life he could understand?

"What does your girl do?"

Christopher answered in sentences whose individual words were intelligible. It was the syntax, the meaning, that fled.

When they came to New York, the road lost all connection with the shape or look of the land. It dived, swung, curved, twisted back on itself, over other roads and under them. Buildings crowded nearer and nearer as in a kinetic hallucination of suffocation, claustrophobia, and spaceless-ness. The commercials between symphonies gave way to a long newscast about Vietnam, New York, Turkey, Israel, Lindsay, Rockefeller and people whose roles and names Stephen could not identify. As usual there was nothing about South Africa. From here it seemed an almost non-existent country. The few Americans who had heard of it refracted it, distorted it, saw it as an image of their own problems. If they cared at all, it was not for a country that had an independent existence, it was for a symbol of their own conflicts. The little of South Africa that survived had been absorbed into the bloodstream of another system. And if he were to survive, he must learn who all these people were, must learn to become interested in them, must tutor himself in this system, this Vietnam, CORE, LSD, FBI, CIA, UCLA, this system of symbols and personalities in whom he had no interest. He must give up his self, and must become a self who could subsist in this vast artifact that offered hardly a blade of grass he could recognize from his own life.

They drove through Harlem. The stores advertised foods he had never eaten. Children played games with rules and passwords he had never known. He had been here, in a black world as foreign as the white, where people didn't understand his English and stared at his strangeness, this black Harlem whose language was as opaque as Spanish Harlem's, as whiteness, as the intelligent assurance of a youth like Christopher.

They left Central Park behind them and the big stores, and came to Stephen's hotel. When Andrew Mohone and Ester Matimba had come to meet him at the airport and offered to help him find accommodation, they had been careful not to take him to Harlem. Andrew wore a loose, flowered costume that he had never worn in South Africa.

He carried an airmail edition of the London *Times* under his arm. Later he explained that many had to masquerade to get a respect they could not otherwise achieve.

"Don't you feel funny to be an African pretending to be an African so that Americans will recognize you as the kind of African they recognize?"

"What sort of game is that, man? You've got to do it. Believe me, there are lots of tricks to learn."

Ester wore the expensive clothes of a performer offstage. Her bearing neither expected nor brooked contempt. And in their aura, Stephen had been able to rent a room out of Harlem.

When Christopher left him, with vaguely friendly American remarks about being glad to meet him, Stephen wondered whether to phone Ester. Or should he wait until this somber mood lightened? He felt lethargic, almost inanimate. He opened the window of his room. It gave onto a dark airshaft. In a corner a heap of crates and cartons rotted and waited for someone to dispose of them. Lights from other rooms in the hotel glowed anonymously. A pale sky sagged against the building's dark bulk. The city's flaccid roar sank toward the rotting corners of the airshaft. Its hoarse wheeze breathed into his face. The outside air, like the air in his room and in the passages of the hotel, had been used so often that an impalpable grime hung in it, like wear in the face of an old prostitute. Any man who took comfort in its warmth breathed dying, as if he slept in a closed room where a brazier breathed.

He took out his notes for the theme of the game under the blanket. The whole affair seemed pitifully thin and worthless, but he tried to work on it. Every new idea seemed banal, false, either involuntarily reminiscent of a commercial, or masquerading like Andrew as an Africa he had never experienced, unnaturally bright and vigorous. Ai! the winter mornings had been cold, the air outside fierce, the water from the tap outside blinding. He and his brother in torn vests hid from the windy sun. Did Andrew tell stories about living in a jungle? Did he wear a different country in his memory and forget the location winters and the cracked European jackets of his native past? Stephen juggled the thin souvenir of those winters he dared not forget, devised harmonies and variations, and eventually put the sheets away. He phoned Ester.

"Stephen! It's good to hear you, man. How *are* you?"

"O.K. How're you?"

"I'm giving a party. Come."

"When? Now?"

"Yes, now. I've got two people from Columbia who've heard your music and want to meet you. Have you done anything new?"

"No."

"Well, they like what they've heard."

"O.K."

"Are you all right, Stephen?"

"Yes. Why not?"

"I must be imagining. Too long since I've seen you. I'd like to see you myself, not just hand you over to those people from Columbia."

"Drop the party and come with me."

"I can't. TV people and journalists are here too. I want you to meet them, Stephen."

"I've just come back. I'm tired. Some other time."

"Stephen, you sound awfully depressed."

"Goodbye, Ester."

He was surprised to find Ester giving a party. Parties were one of Andrew Mohone's tricks, a habit of the exile community. Ester was surely not one of these. She did not make a special, trivial virtue of being South African and different. She met New York on its own terms. She worked. She did not talk about how much she had suffered at home, how rare and sensational her escape had been. She worked. Ken worked. Christopher worked. That was how they survived. But he could not work. He had lost a gear. He had become junk. He was like the rest of the South African clique. He might as well not despise their party.

He showered and changed. He looked in the mirror cynically. What had been the matter, man. He could still live.

He walked through the airless corridor into the streets. Stores offered enticements to millions of people with incomprehensible needs. Windows showed copper pots and wooden bowls, dyed hammocks, colored glass spheres, ceramic fungus, leather waistcoats, books about Zen, posters, and records of Indian ragas. At best his music would cling to this sea ledge with other monstrous forms, curiosities, fads, psychedelia, and would be heard by these bedecked hermaphrodites whose fantastic forms pressed past him with insinuations of contempt, either at his clothes or blackness. This transient hallucination was yet another world, another language. He was lost in an infinity of variations, unconceived possibilities. They all extinguished him. All pressed suffocation. He was nothing. South Africa was nothing. What he had taken as the world omitted a world, an infinity of worlds.

He mounted a bus and rode it passively until the driver told him that he'd have to pay another fare—the bus had completed its route. He climbed off and walked among shabby and indefinite stores. Some screaming children ran in front of him and were rebuked by a screaming woman whose words he could not interpret. He stopped to stare at a window that displayed a French Provincial dining room and bar. Then he walked on again. A man who might have been drunk leaned toward him and asked the time, brother, but he didn't answer, and the man said "Fuck you, nigger." He didn't answer that either. He was near another incessant highway. It roared without rhythm. He came to an overpass. He stopped to stare at the rapid cars, the in-human speed, the implacable concrete legs of another overpass, the din of America. There was only one way. He would accept America. He would throw himself into it, into the breathless air, the machine light. He tightened his hand on the railing and pulled up. The freeway rushed and fled beneath him. He leapt into it.

The Cross

Felix Morriseau-Leroy
Translated by Marie M . B . Racine

This is how it happened
Jesus Christ had to die
No matter what
He just had to die
Pontius Pilate kept saying: no
Caiphas pressured him so much
That the man Jesus was condemned
Since he had not eaten for two days
He was overcome by weakness
Walking up Mount Olive
With two pieces of wood on his back
He kept falling down and getting up
Pilate was watching him with pity
All the Roman soldiers were watching too
When at that time a Black man happened to pass
Simon the Cyrene
A big black man
As big as Paul Robeson
Happened to pass
He looked at the scene through the eyes of a black man
Pilate felt what was in that black man's heart.
He signaled the soldiers
They all fell upon Simon
And mercilessly beat him
Then they ordered him: take up the cross and carry it
Simon picked it up with one hand
He took it from the white man

He ran with it
He started to sing
He began to dance
He danced and sang
He ran up the hill
Leaving everyone behind
He ran down the hill, he sang, danced and danced
He make the cross turn on his head
He threw the cross in the air
He caught it
He passed it through his legs
He threw it in the air
The cross stayed in the air and twirled by itself
Everybody yelled: a miracle, a miracle
The cross came back down
And Simon caught it
He danced his heart out
Before giving it back to Jesus
Ever since that time whenever a cross is too heavy
A burden too great
They tell the black man to bear it.
And then we sing and dance
We beat the drums and play the trumpet
Our backs are strong.
We carry crosses, tote guns
Load cannons, help the white man
Commit crimes, commit sins
Helping to carry everybody's load.

Shoushoun

Felix Morisseau-Leroy

Whenever i have nightmare
i dream of tonton macoutes

The other night

i dreampt i was carrying my coffin on my shoulders
everybody was laughing in the streets of Port-au-Prince

there were nevertheless 2 or 3 boys
who did not laugh

The other night

i dreamt i was digging my grave in the cemetery
everyone was laughing before the tv set

there were however 2 or 3 girls
who did not laugh

even after they shot me dead
in my dream i saw an old woman
who was not at all in a laughing mood
when everybody was showing their teeth

those 2 or 3 boys
those 2 or 3 girls

i won't want to say more than that
for the devil to steal my voice

that old woman
is Shoushoun Fandal
whom the macoutes dragged
to watch the shooting
of her five sons in the street of Grandgosier

Boat People

Felix Morisseau-Leroy
Translated by Jeffrey Knapp

We are all in a drowning boat
Happened before at St. Domingue
We are the ones called boat people

We all died long ago
What else can frighten us
Let them call us boat people

We fight a long time with poverty
On our islands, the sea, everywhere
We never say we are not boat people

In Africa they chase us with dogs
Chained our feet, embark us
Who then called us boat people?

Half the cargo perished
The rest sold at Bossal Market
It's them who call us boat people

We stamp our feet down, the earth shakes
Up to Louisiana, Down to Venezuela
Who would come and call us boat people

A bad season in our country
The hungry dog eats thorns
They didn't call us boat people, yet

We looked for jobs and freedom
And they piled us on again: Cargo—direct to Miami
They start to call us boat people

We run from the rain at Fort Dimanche
But land in the river at Krome
It's them who call us boat people

Miami heat eats away our hearts
Chicago cold explodes our stomach
Boat people boat people boat people

Except for the Indians—
All Americans are immigrants
But it's us they call boat people

We don't bring drugs in our bags
But courage and strength to work
Boat people—Yes, that's allright, boat people

We don't come to make trouble
We come with all respect
It's them who call us boat people

We have no need to yell or scream
But all boat people are equal, the same
All boat people are boat people

One day we'll stand up, put down our feet
As we did at St. Domingue
They'll know who are boat people

That day, be it Christopher Columbus
or Henry Kissinger—They will know
whom we ourselves call people

Dream

Felix Morisseau-Leroy

I am dreaming with eyes open
is it anybody's concern
let me dream with eyes open
I dream in broad daylight
you may say what you like
i like to dream with eyes open
those who cannot dream may not dream
they are not to bother about me
if i like to dream with eyes open
let me dream my dream
some people are rather strange
there are people who never dream
am i asking them to dream
there are people who do not dream of colors
neither red nor green
it is their own affair
my dreams are full of flame trees and hibiscus
full of horses frolicking in pastures of Guinea corn
prancing along paths
with sugar cane both sides
i dream i am walking in gardens
with poinsettia six-months-red in profusion
i dream i am climbing mountains
i am running climbing mountains
after each mountain another mountain
higher to climb
since i was born i have been climbing
the higher the mountain
the smoother they get in my dreams
i am flying climbing mountains

there are people who never dream they are flying
i dream i am flying across rivers
flying across deep dark ravines
i dream i am flying high over the heads of the men-pigs
who cannot see me
i dream i am flying high
leaving the ill-doers far below
i plunge and rub my chest
over the breasts of the hills
why shouldn't i dream as i wish
i dream i am strolling in thick coffee walks red and green
under mango trees laden with golden fruits
in a paradise of mameys
i dream so much with eyes open
that i can't sleep at night anymore
i dream of a brook of clear water
that is like sparkling crystals
where is such a brook to be found
if not on top of Sault du Baril cascade
i dream i am swimming in the sea
of Granddosier Jâcmel l'Anse d'azur Jeremie
in the middle of the corals in Corail
there is no sea like that in any other place
i dream i am shooting pictures
of the coastal cliffs of Anse-a-Pitre
in broad daylight i am dreaming that much
of my islands in carnival
from Cuba through Jamaica to Trinidad
everyone singing and dancing
let me dream my dream
to strengthen my courage
since i know my dream will come true
let me dream my dream

men-pigs – champouel, secret society of men changed into pigs.
mameys – called apricot in Haiti, mamey-apple in Trinidad

Kindergarten

Elzbieta Ettinger

When she fell down, breathless, heavy, all wet, Benjamin's words again sounded in her ears, "Don't try to get out at the cemetery gate; they watch it day and night; be careful not to get lost there." Which she had been. Now she left them far behind. Those people and the gate. And Benjamin too, it struck her suddenly.

From the very beginning he tried to persuade her to renounce the "absurd" idea of leaving the ghetto other than through the sewers. He had a clear liking for the word *absurd* and pronounced it, deliberately drawling, with a contemptuous grimace on his handsome face. He insisted the underground way was the only safe one left: any other was absurd. However, after Sara came back—the only survivor of fourteen who tried to get out through the sewers—Elli knew she would never make it. She was completely terrified listening to Sara's scattered account of the forty-two hours of hopeless struggle in darkness against the waves of thick, quaggy drainage. More than of people, or bullets, or fire, Elli was afraid of choking.

She wanted to get out as she had come in eleven days before—through the wall. The wall worked now the other way around: it kept off the Germans who wouldn't enter the ghetto except through cleared paths and in close order; and it became instead a bulwark and passage for the insurgents. All she needed was darkness. Shelled and battered, the bricks were easy to remove; and any outlet in the open excluded suffocation.

Benjamin argued that within the last six days four out of thirty people who had tried the wall got out alive, whereas over sixty out of eighty got out through the canals. The last unfortunate group did not make him change his mind. He said bluntly that Elli was hysterical about this choking business and that it was better to choke than to fall into their hands.

Only one sewerage outlet was reported from outside to be still safe; it was the one farthest east which took at least sixteen hours to get through. Two others—one coming out right in the middle of a marketplace, the other in a distant suburb, safe only a few days ago—were already useless. Watched day and night by German guards and volunteering hoodlums, they had turned into actual traps. Abel reported from outside that both the guards and the Poles could now rarely be bribed. He said they enjoyed the game more than the money and strongly advised against taking this chance. The fun of the game, he explained impatiently to the amazed Benjamin, lay in surprising the people emerging from the ditch; they called it "pull-push." The point was to give a helping hand to the emerging person, pull him out, and at the moment he grasped the situation, to push him back and snap the iron lid down.

Benjamin insisted that Elli join the group of four, Leo and his wife Klara, Ala and Noah, and try the east sewer. He felt it was a far better chance for her than to go by herself through the deserted streets, where any errant bullet could hit her. Half-heartedly Elli agreed; and then Sara came back. That was when Benjamin told her, "Let me think for you, let me be reasonable for you." He was right that her brains did not work any longer. If she still knew anything, it was that her mind was a complete blank. She could almost physically feel the vacuum in her head. She reacted to Benjamin's arguments like an automaton, repeating dully, "I would choke, I would choke," so that at last Benjamin gave up. He told her she would never get out alive; and if she felt her instinct was right, she was

91

mistaken. She did not know whether she felt anything, instinct or not, and she nodded approvingly when he shouted angrily that she could have just as well chosen a less absurd way of committing suicide.

The group of four left at dusk. Without Elli. It was a cloudy but warm May day. Moshe, the eleven-year-old guide, brought them to the sewer outlet. He was back late in the afternoon. He reported that the usual twenty-minutes' distance took them almost three hours; they had to wait twice for "enemy patrols" to pass, then a mortar shell exploded almost under their feet. Then, they again had to wait to make sure nobody was within hearing distance. This was not simple at all; Moshe scratched his head, his red-rimmed eyes weary and serious in his freckled sweating face. Explosions, detonations and fire, and howling dogs and hungry rats, could mislead the most sensitive ear. Finally, he saw them descend into the inlet. On his way back he was stopped only once by the sound of a shell-fire he could not place. It was clear Moshe was very concerned with Benjamin's estimation of his assignment and reconnaissance. Benjamin looked at him sternly, shook his hand when the boy finished, then told Sara to feed him. He did not say anything to Elli but looked at her with bitter and accusing eyes while the boy was talking. Then they sat silent on the basement floor, leaning against the damp wall. Elli was dozing, her head on Benjamin's shoulder, while he scribbled something on small sheets of crumpled paper in the dim light of the candle.

At quarter-past three it grew light. Elli got up, stiff and cold from sitting motionless on the concrete, wrapped herself tighter in her coat, and said to Benjamin, "I will go now, Benjamin. I know my coming here and my leaving are equally senseless but I never had much sense. Don't be angry, please."

She did not wish him good luck; every word implying his survival would have sounded like an insult. He did not wish her good luck either. He told her to keep close to the walls, to stop at full daylight, wait in hiding until dusk. Then he said, "Don't try to get out near the cemetery gate; they watch it day and night. Be careful not to get lost there." He squeezed the crumpled sheets of papers into her hand, hugged her, lightly kissed her on the lips, and pushed her toward the door.

She left and never looked back, not even once. Not that she was afraid she might yield and change her mind, or might once more experience the compulsion of going back to stay with them till the very end. She was only afraid she might see somebody following her. She was more frightened of facing a man than of what he could do to her. A bullet in her neck was all he could do. She preferred to get it unannounced.

The moment she heard the basement door slam behind her, her mind started to work. She experienced a funny feeling, as if something clicked in her head and put her brain back in motion. She felt it defrosting, receptive. Again she was able to think clearly, the first time since Benjamin told them the fight was lost. Completely alert, she repeated silently his last instructions, jumping over scattered glass, broken pieces of furniture, half-burned bricks. She tried to keep as close as possible to the shattered houses; whenever this shelter—which was like a live thing moving, squeaking, swaggering—became too noisy, hinting danger, she would move farther toward the open, straining her ears and eyes. She felt defenseless and awkward without her glasses which had gotten smashed in battle two days before; her blinking, shortsighted eyes twice spotted at a far distance a green-gray uniform. Once it turned out to be a curtain dangling from a broken sash;

once, a green-painted bathtub shamelessly exposed on the fourth floor of a split house. Waiting for each to aim at her, she lost at least half an hour both times.

It was six by her watch when she decided to stop. The day was bright and sunny, much too bright and much too sunny; a cloudy one would have given her one hour more in the morning and one at night. She had to wait now about twelve hours. She could not make out where she was; she had never been in this part of the ghetto before; and besides, the streets were a jungle of stones and bricks, impossible to tell one from the other. She guessed she had come about two-thirds of the way. Benjamin told her the trip should take her no more than four hours; deducting the lost sixty minutes, she had been walking for about two hours. She planned to start around seven at night; at nine she should reach the Aryan side.

She hid behind an iron gate in a huge, burned-out red brick apartment building. From behind the iron bars she looked outside. For the first time she took a closer look at the area through which she had passed blind, attentive only to danger. She did not realize before how dead a dead city can be. Now she fixed her eyes upon the monstrous piles of charred bricks, melted iron, broken pipes, smoldering wood. And she prayed and demanded that this fiery desert reduced to dust and ashes had never been a man's home. Or, at least, not for a very, very long time. A year, or a half year, or, oh God, a month. Until she saw the first corpse, then a second, then a third. She closed her eyes and cried listlessly.

Then she fell asleep and upon waking, feeling her hand being touched, almost fainted. Her scream came short and shrill. She opened her eyes and saw a small boy standing close to her, gently stroking her hand. Before she came to her senses, the boy said in one breath, "I'm nine; I only look so small; my name is Isaak. Can you give me some-

94

thing to eat?" Dumbfounded, she reached into her pocket and gave him the parcel which Sara had put there last night.

But he was more experienced. "Let's divide it," he said. "You will be hungry too and you will find nothing to eat here. I have searched all over already. You know, I have lived here for a long time, and for the last two days I couldn't find a thing. Nothing, would you believe it, nothing at all."

He said all this so unemotionally that it made her blood run cold. His eyes shone with sincerity; his little face was patient, earnest. She felt nothing but a cold hurt despair; she was numb, heavy with dull pain. The boy, meanwhile, slowly unfolded the newspaper, with his dirty thin fingers gathered the overflowing marmalade from both sides of the crust, smeared it over the piece of bread lying on the palm of his left hand, meticulously measured it with the thumb and forefinger of the right, marked it in the middle with his nail, and broke it in two. One half he put in the pocket of a soiled, torn, adult-sized jacket, hanging loosely on him, the other he wrapped again in the newspaper to give back to Elli. He stood for a while, the small parcel in his outstretched hand. Seeing he was waiting vainly, he put it in the pocket of her coat. Elli stood, unable to move, to utter a word. The boy did not seem to be bothered by her.

Once more he gently touched her hand and said, "I must go now. I left my little brother over there." He pointed with his hand toward the nearby ruins. "Must feed him. He is always hungry and crying. You know how it is with children, they never understand a thing." He did not look at her; nor did he seem to expect any answer. Suddenly he knelt down, picked up Elli's glove, and tucked it into the other pocket of her coat. He turned toward the inner yard and started to go. Elli wanted to call him back, to say something to him, to give him the rest of the bread, but she could not utter a word. When still a child, she had experienced this feeling of frustrating impotence: she had been drowning and could not make herself cry for help. Now also she opened and closed her mouth like a fish searching for water, but no sound came from her throat. The sight of the tiny creature disappearing from the yard made her somehow move. She started to go slowly, then she ran after him. She had the sticky parcel in her outstretched hand. The boy did not turn. He could not see her. She could not call him. She saw the small figure diving into what might have been a store on the ground floor; then he emerged, desperately small now, on a heap of iron pipes. He stopped there for a minute, as if gathering breath, then jumped down and disappeared completely.

Unsure of what to do next, Elli stopped. Then she went slowly across the yard up to the smashed store entrance. Inside, water was dripping from a broken faucet; the floor was covered several inches deep. She turned and went back to the iron gate. She still could not voice a sound. Collapsed on the ground, she tried hard to say something aloud. She tried with "mother," then with "God," then with "father." Her lips moved but no sound came out. Then she recalled that the first word children say is "mama," and she tried this. Again she failed.

At half-past six Elli got up, combed her hair, straightened the crumpled coat. She took the piece of bread out of her pocket, put the small parcel exactly in the same place where the boy found her, and fastened it with a brick. To make sure he would find it, she took the beige glove he had picked up, put it on the brick, and placed a stone on the top. She left the gate, turned left, stopped, went back to the gate, and silently stared at the funny small pyramid. It was so silent that she could hear the dripping water across the yard. Suddenly her fingers felt something hard in her pocket and she knew it was the mint Abel had given her before he left. She put it into the glove, once more fastened it with the stone, and left.

She had been walking for perhaps an hour when she saw something glittering in the fading sunshine. Uneasy, nervously blinking, she moved forward a little. Right in front of her, at a distance of perhaps one hundred yards, there was a barbed-wire-edged cemetery fencing. At the same time she heard loud voices, laughter, shouting. And a trumpet in her head, "Be careful not to get lost there." Her palms and armpits were cold and wet. The pit of her stomach was hollow. She was afraid. Rigid, stiff, hardly breathing, there she stood, facing the gate, till it grew completely dark. Sometime later, perhaps as long as an hour, the voices died away. When she became aware of the silence she started to go.

She took a few steps, stopped, made sure nobody was following her, and then, delirious, lunatic, blind, took flight. She kept running until she fell down, Benjamin's words in her ears.

An acute pain in the elbow and in the knee brought her back to life. She touched the knee. It was swollen and sticky but she could straighten her leg. She was dying to light the last cigarette she had, but frightened it might draw somebody's attention. She lifted her head and saw a lamppost; this was what she had fallen upon. She crawled to it, leaned her aching back against it, and looked around. No ruins, no flames, no smoke, nothing she was familiar with. What part of the ghetto was she in? Which part was still intact? Benjamin said not one street was left, not one house; he must have been wrong. Her confusion growing, she stared at the smooth asphalt road glittering in the moonlight. A small kite was dangling on a birch. Not far behind stood a one-family house, then another, and another. None of this belonged to the dead city. She realized she had crossed its border.

Elli spent the rest of the night sitting on a log under the birch tree. When she sat down, she instantly fell asleep. Later in the night the cold and barking dogs woke her up. A nauseous feeling in her stomach reminded her that she had eaten for the last time when Moshe came back to the basement. She did not feel hungry, but rather dizzy. She stretched out flat on the ground and with her face touching the earth lit the cigarette, carefully shading the flame with the palm of her hand. She was careful not to inhale too deeply on an empty stomach. She still had half of the cigarette, the glowing end down, in her folded palm when the well-known, heavy pace of nailed boots reached her. She crushed the cigarette in her palm and lay still. When the patrol passed, she said aloud and absentmindedly, "Oh, mama." After a long while she realized that her hand was badly burned and that she could talk.

Caracas

Tibor Tollas
Translated by Marguerite Guzman Bouvard

Like an Indian maiden, the city basks
in the warm sunset, resting her lovely head
on the mountain's velvety green pillows.
I whisper her name, Caracas.

Her faithful lover, eternal summer,
fastens purple orchids in her dark locks.
The blue Caribbean caresses
her sun-dappled knees with frothy hands.

The sun plunges into the ocean
like an enormous blazing ball.
Suddenly night falls with its dark,
jeweled robes. The city lights
awaken in sparkling throngs.

The people are gathering; the mountain
chants its love to the Indian maiden
with words learned from the old conquistadores.
She is watched by ancestors and hushed centuries.

Prayer for a Peaceful Death

Tibor Tollas
Translated by Marguerite Guzman Bouvard

O Lord, who has suffered,
I beseech you, not for life,
but for the grace of a peaceful death.
Let it come suddenly, without warning,
like sleep, like sunset.
Let no cruel pain or memories
furrow my darkening face
as it looks into the long night.
May I never become a burden,
pity only weighs me down.
With my head high, I want
to drink up the sun,
with a thousand arms,
I want to reach up,
and die standing, like the trees.

Summer's End

Tibor Tollas
Translated by Marguerite Guzman Bouvard

I want to find you again
under the shimmering chestnut trees
of slow September afternoons.
Like branches filling with light,
I want to warm in your presence,
and with the trees, listen to your voice.

I put my weary arms around your shoulders,
musing on long gone days.
We can't bring them back,
but we have a few years left,
a short space ahead.
I want to cross it with you,
let your smile fill me.

Who knows when frost will take us.
I want to blaze like the sun
pouring out its final gold.
I want to stride ankle-deep in the wet grass
and vanish against the horizon.
One more flourish, like trees at the end of summer.

The Trees in my Orchard

Tibor Tollas

Translated by Marguerite Guzman Bouvard

No one can uproot the trees
of my childhood.
I'll carry the burdens
of those leafy crucifixes
until I reach my destination.

I'll taste the sweet juice
of pears until I die.
Grandmother holds them out
from her bulging apron,
from fifty years ago.

The heavy limbs of the plumtrees
offer their blue treasures
for my table.

The cherries' purple
moistens my parched tongue.
Haunting memories of my youth
quench my thirst.

I'll carry the orchards
of my childhood through the years.
No one can disturb
a single branch, a fragrant bloom.

The Bend in the River Danube

Tibor Tollas
Translated by Marguerite Guzman Bouvard

*At the penitentiary town of Vac, in central Hungary, the Danube
River, after having flowed six hundred miles east toward Russia,
turns sharply and irrevocably south and makes its way to the
Euxine by way of Hungary, Yugoslavia, Bulgaria, and Rumania.
This is "the big bend" which Tibor Tollas makes the symbol of an
avoidance of doom in Soviet tyranny. He pleads rather for
fellowship in freedom among all the peoples of the Danube
Valley.*

Watson Kirkconnell

Beyond the doors, the mountains
slowly fan out.
Like tombstones of bygone times,
they do not worry about tomorrow.

The sombre gray prison with its steely eyes
bathes in the Danube
but the river curves through the shadowy land
with a centuries-old indifference.

It carries memories of battles,
of agonies and passions
while the lives of its ill-fated sons
smother in dungeons.

King of rivers, queen of tiny nations,
beloved valley, for a thousand years
you were our home, the boundary of Europe.
Embrace us with a mother's loving arms,

not as a cruel border which divides and separates,
like the iron bars on our windows,
like hatred. We cling to each other,
prisoners, caught between enemies.

Gazing at the river as it bears the light
from West to East, we can see the bend,
how suddenly it veers then journeys south,
leaving the east behind.

The ancient river points out the way
to the small, angry nations on its banks.
It tells them that they must unite.
The centuries demand it.

From the narrow windows of our cells,
we can see the future
where the blood-rich soil sings victoriously.
Don't look right or left. Stand fast, this is your land.

River of nations, ferry our clear convictions
throughout the valleys.
Let our faith nourish the banks
until gardens spring up

with the fruits of two worlds.
Cleanse our spirits so that we meet
and hold each other
as brothers living in one valley.

There is no other way.
The seas of West or East may call us,
but the Danube draws in our fleeting streams.
Brother, outside this valley you are lost.

104

Hear our message from the bend in the Danube.
Take our outstretched hands,
let our common fate, our shared suffering
conquer arrogance and hate.

The tributaries of the Danube gather
in this valley. Let us go forth,
the aching times demand it.
We will win our freedom, each distinct, but united.

In the Whirlwind

Tibor Tollas

Translated by Marguerite Guzman Bouvard

In the whirlwind of scourging times,
we are the storm-tossed branches and leaves,
the dead, the prisoners, the refugees.
We seek the tree, seek our roots.

We clung to barbed wire with bleeding hands
and our bare feet froze to the Don's
icy skin. We were scattered
to the four corners of the world.

Those who remained among the ruins
cowered like grass in the wind.
The sky was taken from them,
their past, cancelled.

Nine springtimes of my life vanished
behind wind struck walls.
But there came an Autumn,
and its nine days repaid us.

In a foreign land, the sky
once more belonged to me, its nine stars
sparkling in my heart. The trees
I loved, those old friends from home,
journeyed with me.

Nine stars glimmer in my hands.
Now we carry the nine flames of hope.
We light a fire in the night
where the darkness is its darkest.

On the Continental Divide

Tibor Tollas
Translated by Donald Hall

I am caught on the ridge of a mountain range.
Around us there are oceans on both sides.
Our waters look for a way to flow
To the sloping plains of East and West.
I am standing on the wall of centuries
And keep watch like the last soldier
At his post in the destruction of Pompeii.
Both of these oceans touch our shores.
A man is Hungarian
As long as he belongs to neither of them.

Where the Cloister Stood

Tibor Tollas
Translated by Hal Smith

The lime trees used to flower there
And a white monk kneeled through the garden
Saying his prayer of weeding out the roses.
The roses talked back to him
And water was a word he understood.

It is the same place
Ruined and a prison
Damp and brittle to your nails.

But take your tortured hands
And scratch out your poems.
Stone will last longer than paper.

Europe is burning its shame into your walls.

Memento

Tibor Tollas
Translated by John Knoepfle

The window of the great basilica
composes the rays of the sun.
Saints become gold in the window.
They are silent, turning
the pages of your dream.

Solemnity fills this church.
It surrounds the kneeling women.
Even the Good Lord reads here.
He reads the secret folios of your soul,
and he smiles.

You bow your head in devotion
and a flower falls from your hair.
I think, for a moment, that God is sad,
your flower in the aisle at my feet.

An old memento.
O fragrant and pure sweet petals!

Creatures of Land and Water

Tibor Tollas
Translated by James Wright

I draw on my diving gear,
My blanket, and sink down.
My net of language drifts back up, behind me.
Far down, leaves yield their damp shadows wide open
To my hands' ripples in the darkness.

Down there, behind closed shells,
Treasures have lain, blinded, for a thousand years.
When I swim past, mother-of-pearl flares
Fire through the dumb lips.

My hands tremble, as I lift up
The jewels of that night.
Hurry, hurry, string them on sentences
(God whispers to me).

I carry them back toward the light, these riches
I stole from a deep place.
It's no use. One word, and the whole fire
Falls to gray ashes, and the pearls scatter
Back into the sea.

You Can't Get There from Here

Ludmila Shtern
Translated by Bill Tjalsma

Say, friend, why so harassed?
Do you think of anything but Paris?
—*Yurakukin*

Humming these words early one morning in 1970, I flew down the stairs, late for work as usual.

Imagine a dark Leningrad morning, the coming day promising nothing but socialist obligations, with payday still three days off, the warty face of department chief Comrade Pypin looming in your mind's eye. What can the mail possibly bring on such a morning?

I opened the mailbox. A bunch of bills fluttered to my feet, the magazine *Woman Worker* and a strange letter—a pale lilac envelope, encrusted with seals and scarlet crests.

My foreign uncle was inviting me to visit him in France. Of course, no one ought to be surprised at receiving official papers from abroad today. If the envelopes containing invitations to Israel were laid like white tiles they would cover the whole of European Russia. But in the year nineteen-*seventy*, an invitation from the municipality of Paris, sealed with wax, rattled me more than a communication from a flying saucer.

I called my office, and, fighting the exultation that choked me, disconsolately informed Comrade Pypin of a sudden gall bladder attack. Less than an hour later, I was dashing over to OVIR, the Passport and Registration Office. These days, the OVIR waiting room is as overcrowded as Red Square during the anniversary of the Revolution. But then, in 1970, the place was as empty and silent as a Buddhist temple.

I was interviewed by a stout blond man with a brass basin in place of a face, called Kabashkin. Giving a virtuoso imitation of a smile, he motioned to a chair, shoved the ashtray in my direction and buried himself in the study of my invitation. When Kabashkin finally raised his eyes, his brass basin glowed softly.

"When would you prefer to travel?"

I was so taken aback that I lost the gift of speech. Such a considerate question caught me unawares.

"I don't know . . . as soon as possible, that is . . . when I receive permission . . ." I squeezed out.

"I personally feel that spring is the best time," he said dreamily.

"Spring, you think?" I inquired dully.

"Spring, spring . . . Everything in bloom there then."

Violins began singing; the room filled with the aroma of flowering chestnuts and acacia. My natural suspiciousness cracked like March ice.

"Would it be possible sooner? For instance, this winter?"

"Why not? It's beautiful there in winter, too. Only, I can't say whether they have snow in Paris, then," Kabashkin said anxiously.

"Will there be time to make out the papers?"

"Why not? The tourist season is over, and everything that depends on us personally we'll finish in time."

Above his brass basin a golden nimbus appeared. We chatted a bit more about Paris, establishing the presence of the Louvre and the Eiffel Tower there, and parted reluctantly. In saying goodbye, the instructor handed me some questionnaires: Form No. 6, Form No. 86, Form No. 1003.

"You'll be able to get the information and fill out the

questionnaire without difficulty? The sooner the better," murmured Kabashkin.

The pile of forms was so thick I had to hold them in both hands. I backed off toward the exit, muttering:

"Thanks, thank you very much, thank you . . . I appreciate it."

Going out into the autumn slush, I took a deep breath, did thirty-two *fouettees,* and strode decisively down the alluring path to Paris.

"Tolya," I said to my husband, "give me a notarized statement that you haven't any objections to my visiting my uncle."

"What's with you? Why should I object?"

"OVIR wants to know that you're giving me permission to go to Paris while you are in sound mind and not under hypnosis or the influence of narcotics. That's in Form 86."

"Oh, if it's No. 86, that's a different matter," said Tolya respectfully. "Tomorrow I'll take time off and drop by a notary's. I won't be needing a note from my psychiatrist, will I?"

"You, no, but I will, for sure. And from a dozen doctors as well . . ."

"Right. And don't forget to drop by the coroner's office. His autopsy might well be the deciding factor."

In the morning, I raced over to my Apartment Administration Office. Naturally, they were not receiving that day, but in exchange for a pair of imported pantyhose, the clerk typed out Form No. 6 regarding the number of people in my family.

By evening, I had in my possession two documents. Inspired by this initial success, I bought a folder, wrote "France" on it with a red pencil and laid the groundwork for Paris.

Next, an assault on the polyclinic was undertaken. Rushing from window to window in the waiting room, I finagled passes that got me into offices ahead of the queue. My organism was studied by an orthopedist and a phthisiologist, a urinologist and a neurologist. I choked down a rubber tube and swallowed barium. I rushed down crowded corridors, modestly trying to conceal the containers I was carrying. I stood in front of and lay down under powerful X rays. They even stuck a red light in my rear, which gave me the look of the new model Volga sedan.

Not two weeks went by before the doctors decided unanimously that so far as my internal organs were concerned there was no reason I couldn't take a trip. One detail remained—the chief doctor's check mark. He raised his pen, but suddenly it froze ominously in the air.

"What about the venereologist? I don't see the venereologist's signature."

"Do you really think . . . could you even suppose that . . ." I began on a high note but was interrupted by a mercilessly logical question:

"Tell me, why should we take your word for it?"

There was no answer to that question, and I retreated, downcast.

At the regional dermatological and venereological dispensary I presented myself before the doctor. She was severe and glum, maintaining an infinite distance from sexual problems.

"Sign this slip for abroad," I shot out boldly.

"What do you mean, 'Sign this!'" the doctor said in astonishment. "We don't sign anything just like that. We'll take some smears and you'll get a response in three days."

"Smears? What for?"

"Gonorrhea, whatever—we'll see what you've got there . . ."

"I've got gonorrhea? What about syphilis?"

"Maybe syphilis, too," the venereologist nodded her head.

"Are you serious? This is ridiculous . . . it's got to be a joke."

"I advise you not to be too quick to laugh, patient. If, patient, you accidentally turn out to be healthy, then laugh all you want."

Three days later, it was determined that "the patient does not suffer from any of the following venereal diseases . . ."

"And so, physically, you are suitable," said my husband approvingly. "What about your moral health? You think it'll pass?"

The question was far from frivolous. My ideological preparedness to go see my uncle had to be attested to by a recommendation from my employer that had to be approved by the Regional Committee of the Party.

"Who could write me a recommendation for abroad?" I appealed to Comrade Pypin, just glimpsing a fleeting smile on his face. It disappeared among the innumerable wrinkles on his cheeks.

"Run over to the Trade Union Committee. The girls there have the right forms."

The new secretary raised her Botticelli eyes.

"What do you want? To be released on bail or get on the list for a co-op?"

"No . . . Going abroad."

"Socialist or capitalist?"

"To a capitalist country!"

She provided me with a sheet whose last line read: "Administration, Party Committee and Trade Union Committee recommend Comrade (blank) for a trip to (blank) and bear responsibility for this recommendation." In the corridor I read the entire text. If they checked off all virtues ennumerated therein, I could easily be selected for the Supreme Soviet or even take an honored place in a funerary urn beside the Kremlin wall.

Once I had obtained all the signatures and had the form

stamped with an official seal by way of decoration, I prepared for my interrogation by the Regional Committee. A schoolmate of mine, now head of the university's dialectical materialism department, dragged over to my apartment whole sets of *Communist*, and *New Times*, and a pile of Party propagandists' instruction manuals. Inspired by slugs of cognac, he explained the significance of the last Party Congress and of certain key speeches. Finally, I gulped down a tranquilizer and set out for my interview, whispering to myself the names of the Communist leaders of the nation, and of the heads of nations belonging to NATO.

The Regional Committee was housed in the former mansion of the Gagarin princes. Marble cupids aimed their arrows at me; crystal chandeliers glimmered blue and rose; the stairway was covered with scarlet carpet. Tropical plants swayed over the plaster-skull of the Founder of the First Socialist Country in the World.

In the waiting room there was already a crowd of about ten people. An architect who had been invited to put up something grandiose in Morocco was nervously making notes in a copybook; two junior professors who were being sent to temporarily friendly Ghana were flipping through *Party Life*; the members of a musical quartet—heralds of Soviet culture in Finland—chattered by the window.

A group of comrades headed for business trips disappeared beyond massive oak doors; when they reappeared, their crimson faces, which looked as if they had just come out of a sauna, revealed nothing about whether or not permission had been granted for them to spread art and scientific and technical progress. Finally it was my turn. Thirteen important people sat imposingly around a table to question me. I perched modestly on the edge of a chair.

"The comrade has received an invitation from France to visit her uncle," the second secretary, Guzin, began. "Are there any questions for the comrade?"

117

"How is your uncle related to you?" asked a flaccid lady without a neck.

"He is my uncle," I answered firmly.

"Could you specify in what sense?"

"In the sense that he is my mother's brother."

"Interesting. How did your uncle end up in France?" The words resounded from the side somewhere.

"His parents moved there when he was a child," I responded with a note of censure. Twenty-six eyes looked at me reproachfully.

"At what age?" Guzin asked severely.

"At three," I said, taking two years off Uncle's age at the time, hoping it would mitigate his criminal act.

"And when did this occur?"

"1916 . . . a year before the Revolution," I moved even further back in time.

"So why go see him if you don't even know him?"

"I do know him; he visited the USSR."

"Then why go see him if you know him?"

Actually, why? I didn't have a single argument in my head.

"Hmmm . . . I want to meet his family and . . . see France."

"That's interesting," an old man representing the Soviet of Retired People put it nastily. "So you've seen everything in your own country?"

"Of course not," I responded politely, "but, you see, my uncle isn't here."

"Have you ever visited a capitalist country?" asked someone thin and apparently jaundiced.

"No . . . not yet. This would be the first time."

"There, you see . . ." he exulted, baring teeth the color of khaki. "You've got no experience traveling in capitalist countries. Better to start with a socialist country, say, for example, Bulgaria."

"In principle, you are absolutely right," I agreed respectfully, "but my uncle, in a certain sense, lives in France . . . as it happens."

"Under what auspices did he visit here? If it's not confidential."

"He's a film director."

"Is he famous?" The lady without a neck looked jealous.

"I should say so!" I said cruelly, then pulled myself together and specified: "And very progressive."

"Tell me, please, how interesting," she started, clucking. "Does he happen to know Yves Montand?"

I was getting ready to tell her that he was a sort of uncle to Montand too, but Comrade Guzin snorted at the lady and pronounced:

"Your familial situation is clear. But are you sufficiently acquainted with the economic and political situation in France?"

"I think so."

"Don't forget that you will be meeting people and that the Soviet people as a whole will be judged according to your behavior. Do you understand your responsibility?"

After this question, the inquisitor knitted his brows and got down to business. I realized that now, after the curtain-raiser, the real show was beginning.

"What is the party makeup of the coalition government in France?" "What is the comparative production of steel and electrical energy in the USA, England, France and the Benelux countries?" "Why was Roger Garaudy expelled from the French Communist Party?"

"Why? What for? Which?" I felt like a fly beating against a window under the blows of a dishtowel.

When I had answered questions about puppet governments of Latin America and the military operations in the Parrot's Beak and the Fishhook, I felt the onset of cardiac arrest. Something crimson floated before my eyes; my ears popped as if I were in a plane.

"Are you aware that Nixon personally visited the American Sixth Fleet?" The words sounded as if they had come from a closet. "Your comments?"

"Get out of our Mediterranean!" I was on the verge of howling, but I restrained myself and repeated the views of Comrade Krupitsin in yesterday's *Izvestiya*.

Silence followed. Outside through the windows, the street lights were coming on along the embankment. Guzin glanced at his watch and shot out:

"Well, then, do we approve the comrade's application?" (In half an hour, the Czechoslovakia-USSR hockey match would be starting on television.)

The Commission voted and I reeled down the stairs, all but sliding into the tropical plants.

The next morning, my fat folder "France" was conveyed to OVIR.

"You managed that quickly enough," grinned Kabashkin. "With dispatch."

"I hope that my application will not be held up here either," I said brazenly.

Kabashkin's brass basin expressed perplexity:

"I don't make those decisions. I'm only a clerk. But meantime, get ready, don't waste time."

I hadn't been wasting it. Preparing for a goodbye party, our refrigerator already contained an 800-gram can of black caviar I had obtained from the waiter Kolya at the Astoria Restaurant, in exchange for a Beatles album.

"If they don't let you out I hope that we'll be able to eat it, just the two of us," repeated my husband.

Each time he said it I felt a chill. Meantime, friends kept calling, asking me to buy things for them in France. In exchange, they offered woolen scarves from Orenburg, silver tea glass holders, dried mushrooms, lace, semiprecious stones from the Urals, wooden spoons, plus a selection of folk music instruments, including an oversize 13th century balalaika.

Three months passed. Snow came and went, and OVIR was quiet as Lenin's tomb. My heart sank at the thought that the Parisian chestnut trees had blossomed without me. So, plucking up my courage, I called Kabashkin.

"Unfortunately, there's no answer," he intoned into the phone like a velvet cello. "But the minute we hear, we'll let you know."

Finally, a yellowish slip with an invitation to appear arrived. The day before, Mama had won at Patience three times, and a black cat that was about to cross my path had suddenly made a furtive dash into an entryway without the slightest reason. All bespoke success, and I spent a sleepless night, before setting off for OVIR to get there exactly at nine o'clock.

Kabashkin again showed himself to be a miracle of gallantry. He offered me a chair and shoved the ashtray over.

"I must inform you," his brass basin glowing again, "that . . . your trip to France has been turned down. Your documents will remain with us," said he, patting the folder tenderly.

"Why?" I expelled all the air from my lungs.

"That's the way it is. If you wish to apply again, you will have to fill out new forms."

"But why was I turned down?" I asked in a whisper. I had no sensation of the chair beneath me.

"Your uncle is not considered to be a sufficiently close relative."

"What should I do now?"

"Try applying a year from now," Kabashkin said, shrugging his shoulders, obviously tired of the conversation.

"But a year from now he won't be any closer!" I exploded.

"That's logical," he perked up. "Quite logical, even."

"But what should I tell Uncle?" I wasn't getting any calmer. "How can I explain. He won't understand a strange reason like that."

"Why should he? He doesn't have to know. Show some flexibility. Write him that you're swamped with work, that you're on the brink of a scientific discovery, that you're sick . . ." he offered the usual formulas listlessly.

"I'm sick? With what?" I suddenly heard myself crying. "What illness do I have? Gonorrhea? Syphilis?"

Kabashkin's brass basin darkened. He rounded the table, went up to the door and held it open for me. I ended up in the reception room. Behind my back, his caressing voice murmured to the secretary:

"Next, please, sweetheart."

Ezidimma

Ifeanyi Menkiti

Is it for me to call
her by her name, she
at whose command
the air is blessed tonight
and the roads lie without
the slightest ounce of perturbation

Ezi di mma?

Or is it for me to hold
back from all such mention
of her name and let
what is sheltered rest
as such with the dew
as Onitsha moves this day in mind's sight

Ezi di mma?

Adaiba

Ifeanyi Menkiti

The clear stream in the clear day
shall flow with her return;
and may the glow escort her,
as I rise to meet her;
the deep one girt with god-light.

The Little Children

Ifeanyi Menkiti

A goat without fingers
scratching her udders
rubs her udders
against a tree trunk.

The little children think it is funny—
    they say the goat is crazy
    for pressing her udders
    against a tree trunk

The little children watch and laugh.

All Quiet on Slave Row

Ifeanyi Menkiti

Nor could they tell
whether the Negro
was a man
or was somewhere
between an antelope
and a man.

• •

We danced on the ephemera
the ephemera danced with us;
we and the ephemera were one.

Lord of joy
and intermingled blessedness

Jerusalem was builded there
among the dark-set sea.

Arabs came,
the Jews before them;

but, here in our authentic
southern sea, we wept

and spat the seeds
of watermelon—

jolly niggers
come to town.

And there was this adult pain
down deep in the soul

because of which
was laughter.

Lord of tears
and perspiratory blessedness

we shook, we shook
to the rhythm of juba.

Ancestral Ray

Ifeanyi Menkiti

Ancestral ray
                    fell in the grove of forebears;
shaft of amber light
                    among hillocks of the dead city;
ripened at night
                    over the creeping centuries.

And there'll be yet another day,
the one in the wilderness eating with eagles;
and glow of consecrated light
seen with the footfall of the panther;
halo on halo in hallowed grove.

So shall the flame go forth once more
                    in kindled tongues;
so the one dove brood over the abyss,
recumbent over memory;
Aroli, your days within this,
to tell my uncatalogued years.

Age of the Gods

Ifeanyi Menkiti

Age of the gods who never came,
the rose calling, hinting, never blooming;
in season, out of season,
trailing the secret hours;
Son of man, son of man . . .

Singer, in the dark fields
what means this burning of darkness?
and what this motion of closed years?
this projection through time is still dance?
What mean?

Son of Man,
the kingdom of God is within you,
the kingdom of God is also moving,
onward and upward, in stillness,
                    into stillness.

And water also will burn
nor will I be not willing
            to tell of this
when my song of flame is ended -

Who moved among the astral marshes,
tongue-tied, still chanting in the night.

The Long Journeys

Ifeanyi Menkiti

I.

That man was evolved from the fish
we've certainly pondered but do not relish
even if it's been served on the academic dish;
knowing but wishing we we did not know
these slimy beginnings
the marine pregnancies
and Darwin's sea cousins—

       you interstellar ramjets
       fly swiftly till we meet our Dog
       swiftly, O swiftly fly.

II.

These muffled thoughts have swept
       on me upon the waters;
let no ashes be strewn,
       when the eagles are abroad;
for we will go when and whenever death strikes,
       bearing memories of the sundered day.
and we will go when and whenever time calls,
       trailing what secret aeons bring.

Echoes of the deep
where island waters touch the shore;
and all the Haidas gone;
from their summer fishing grounds by the sea all gone;
departed from the staggering surge.

Mist over the waters,
and the wind arrives from Haro,
from Juan de Fuca and Walla Walla
  straight out to sea,
  to the lone last edge of the sea,
  the light house at the end of the point—

  and I call:

    Ikenga, guardian of the ages, protect me;
    by the flood's advance and retreat,
    by the breathing death of the desert beetle,
    the dry infoldings of the scarab twilight,
    in all the twisted, sacred odor of things;
        Protection.

    from the corners of defeat
    and the tremblings at dusk time;
    through these auguries of the deflected light;
        Compassion.

    Compassion;
    lest in these anguished wanderings
    terror strike our thing aghast
    and kill all our little doves.

III.

I brought salt crystals of the auspicious tide
and whatever else the northern new moon shelters:
clear cones and cedars aureate with the sinking sun,
and he who arrives weaving the rainbow in his feet;
as well those things to which anguish had lent its edge,
those that prevent us to speak with confidence of the morn,
the flailing apparitions in the beleaguered nook,
darkness which in the noon-day sun has terrified all,
making the hunter return from his hill before the kill;

A luau or a funeral, and we witness;
yes, we have witnessed the teething corpse;
through time the lament of the few for the lost,
through time the voice of silence from few toward many.

IV.

Then accept these murmurs of man's enduring breath,
and forgive our first offendings, ye gods;
and when the lone light
flickers in the dying daylight,
preserve these untended nurslings;
preserve them and us;
                    before the tulips fold,
                    where night descends,
                    and the lights go out,
                    and spirits pall.

Fish Heads

Ifeanyi Menkiti

Big head of a fish
wet eyes cooking in the pot

O, I love fish-heads
when they simmer

  & white folks
        cannot understand
        why Indians & Africans
        love fish heads,
                eh?—

  in London, the landlady
  got so mad at them
    she threw them
    out of the building
  for cooking fish heads all the time
  and messing up the hallways
            with fish smell

And we have considered the lilies
and how they grow
fed by God's abundant mercy

but the lilies eat manure
and a diet of manure
is not nearly as good
as a diet of fish heads

133

So let the English eat manure
like the lilies in their Bible;

as for us, fish heads when they simmer . . .

The Transformation

Ifeanyi Menkiti

Europeans with their civilization;
Africans confirmed in lechery,
lacking civilization.

Then came Freud and said
  "Fellow Europeans, copulation
  might not be that bad after all."

And now they talk of their new morality
and of the positive assertion of drives
but give no credit to the savages.
Have we not invented lechery?

Europe indeed is changing
America following fast behind—

When all of us shall become confirmed lechers,
the black and the white together,
one riffraff of passion.

Blessed be the Race of Man

Ifeanyi Menkiti

Blessed be the race of man.

Blessed be the Russians
who know the essence of Comradship,
the essence of peaceful coexistence -
   they want to bury the Americans.

Blessed be the Europeans
who bring civilization to backward peoples
and the word of God to them, half-devil, half-child.

Blessed be the Asians
who have shown the wisdom of rice eating
and the peacefulness of Buddha
though the Chinese now say
war is inevitable for the triumph of the Cause
and the uncorrupting of the collective stew.

Blessed also be the Americans
who are very kind to animals
and make trousers for their dogs
and fill the lives of cats with warmth
though their aged die of neglect.

And blessed be the Congolese
who—on the good authority of Time magazine—
eat scrambled nuns.

On Dostoevsky Street

Ludmila Shtern
*Translated by Bill Tjalsma
and Anne Frydman*

It is customary to make communal apartments the subject of horror stories and the object of curses; but sometimes they can be places of idyllic calm. In some cases this state of calm is attained if everyone sharing the apartment takes up transcendental meditation, while in other cases it comes about through a fortunate conjunction of events. In our apartment, the path to silence was cleared by Fate itself.

The events described here took place in Leningrad, at number 32 Dostoevsky Street. Our street was famous for the Kuznechny Open Market and the Yamsky Public Baths. The market disproved the fabrications of Russia's slanderers about the lack of foodstuffs under socialism, and the baths had an intriguing reputation as a hot-bed of sin. In the 1960's it became permissible to recall that Fyodor Dostoevsky himself had lived across from the market, and as a result of this victory by the forces of the intelligentsia over the mighty of the party apparatus, a museum devoted to Dostoevsky opened—with, one might add, no pomp whatsoever.

Our building was always competing to be named "Outstanding Communist Way of Life Building," our stairwell to be named "Outstanding Communist Way of Life Stairwell," and our apartment, in its turn, struggled for the title of "Outstanding Communist Way of Life Apartment." To this end, the parquet in the corridor always shone, but in the kitchen above each table—five in all—an individual twenty-five watt light bulb hung, which revealed our communal adherence to the retrograde idea of privacy and independence.

For many years, our apartment kept up a turbulent but trivial life that did not merit literary attention.

But once, certain events coming one after the other turned our flourishing *kommunalka* into a desert. In our dwelling silence reigned, a silence as deafening as in Levitan's painting "Eternal Peace." This was to come about after the disclosure of an act of treacherous infidelity in the room next to the front door and of murder accomplished in the bathroom.

To the left of the front door lived an engineer from Leningrad Gas, Naum Lvovich Borenboim, and his wife Faina Markovna. Naum was on the stout side, about fifty, moderately bald and moderately roguish. His motto was, "I love you, Life!" Faina, though her husband's age, looked like a representative of an older generation. Gastritis, pancreatitis and other similar surprises of the stomach and intestinal tract had turned her face an ochre hue. Her soul, too, seemed acid with sarcasm.

"That bitch, she only knows to snap or make fun of someone," Senka Roof complained. Senka, a truckdriver, lived across from the room that my family lived in.

"And so backhanded, the underbleached shrew," added Lily, an internal passport clerk from the Housing Office who lived to our right.

All of us in the apartment, though, were only the innocent bystanders of Faina's sardonic remarks. The real target was Naum himself, meek and merry, with light-blue slightly bulging eyes. And everyone could guess why. Naum was unfaithful to her.

It is true that his affairs flowed deep underground—Faina searched furiously for clues, but it was all in vain. She could never find a brassiere in his pocket, or traces of lipstick on his neck, or even a poor little telephone number

138

on a scrap of paper. All the same, vibrations of infidelity could always be felt in the air. The gay deceiver was never unmasked—Borenboim was crafty, and careful.

But once Naum broke the commandment "Thou shalt not sin too close to home," and God's wrath was visited on him that day. Borenboim let his head be turned by his apartment-mate Lily Kuzina, who had thirty years on her shoulders, was indisputably a real blonde and, despite bowed legs that could have been a cavalryman's, was a good-looking girl. Her personal life went on when she went away on vacation to the Black Sea or the Crimea or the Caucasus. Lily's archives preserved the memory of sea captains from Murmansk, union officials from Sverdlovsk, suppliers from Minsk, and even the chief engineer from a toxic chemicals plant in Odessa. Of him Lily said with endearing warmth, "A bit decrepit, of course, but tender and not stingy."

Then it happened that Lily's sober mind prompted her to see that there was no need to go to the ends of the earth when right next door she could find someone a bit decrepit but tender and not stingy in the person of Naum Borenboim. So Lilly dropped some hints that Naum had a chance. Flattered, he made her a present of a bottle of "Red Poppy" perfume and a sprig of mimosa on International Women's Day. On two occasions they snuck off to the movies together. Once Naum asked a friend for his key, and he and Lily spent an afternoon enjoying themselves in a co-op apartment. But for the most part the romance was kept alive very innocently within the limited space of the kitchen, bathroom and corridor, until one time something got into them both and they lost their heads.

It was a warm May evening. Lily was publicly fixing her hair by the mirror in the front corridor. Naum buzzed around her under the pretext of "using the telephone." Coquettishly blowing some hair from her comb in Borenboim's direction, Lily said, "By the way, tomorrow is my

139

birthday. I'm not inviting anybody over—I've had enough of all that. But my girlfriend Tamara has given me a can of crabmeat as a present."

"What can I give you, Lilichka?" Naum asked quickly.

"You yourself, Naum dear. I wish that we could spend the day together. I was even hoping that . . ."

"But where and how?" our Casanova whispered.

"Well, naturally not in public," Lily said, opening her eyes wide, and Naum went numb with desire. Nevertheless, being a realistic man he understood that he would never be able to arrange for a place for them to meet in one day. Then Naum's heated brain produced a brilliant strategic plan. He decided on the following: he would tell Faina that he was being sent on a business trip for two days, and he would pretend to leave for Moscow in the morning. Faina did not like to stay home alone and whenever Naum went on a business trip she would go to stay with her sister. Then Naum would return home in secret and slip into Lily's room where they would drink cognac, feed on crabmeat and give themselves over to love, such as it is. The next morning, taking care not to be seen by the other neighbors, Naum would leave for work and return home officially that evening "from his trip." This plan was put into action at once.

In the morning Naum "left for Moscow." From that moment on, unforeseen snags in the scenario began to appear, and if Borenboim had been a more superstitious person he might have taken warning.

Wandering around a department store during his lunch hour, looking for a birthday present for Lily, Naum by some miracle avoided coming face to face with Faina, who was being pushed and shoved in a line of women waiting to buy henna. Then at the end of the day his boss at work announced that everyone was in for a bonus and that he was taking them all out for drink at the Metropole Restaurant to celebrate. Borenboim quickly said that his wife was sick and that he had to go home.

"What are you worrying yourself about, Naum Lvovich," said his boss, "I'll call up your respected spouse right now and get her approval."

In a moment of panic Naum blurted a lie that the telephone had been disconnected for nonpayment, and, to everyone's amazement, said goodbye and excused himself.

The events that followed are reported below.

7:00 pm. Naum calls the apartment. Lily races to the telephone. "She's gone," she whispers and puts down the receiver.

7:30 pm. Naum enters the apartment through the back door and secretly makes his way to his beloved.

11:00 pm. The light goes out in Lily's room, though music continues to play softly.

11:30 pm. Faina returns home, having had a violent argument with her sister.

3:00 am. Borenboim makes his way to the toilet.

3:05 am. Borenboim heads back from the toilet.

And here an evil spirit—which could also be called a "conditioned reflex"—played a trick on him. Instead of returning to Lily, the sinner, half asleep, mechanically turned into his own room, the one next to the front door.

A soul-rending scream shook the Communist Way of Life Apartment. Awakening from a light sleep, Faina shrieked deafeningly at the sight of a naked man. When she recognized her husband, her voice lifted an octave.

Everyone turned on their lights and all of us poured into the corridor. Senka Roof celebrated as though it was Victory Day and kicked on the Bochkins' door to invite them to share in the festivities. Dressed in Naum's present, a nightgown from East Germany, and looking like a young Greta Garbo, Lily stood stock still, tragically covering her mouth with her palm. Poor Naum was hopping from one foot to

141

the other in the center of the storm, clutching his head and sputtering, "Oh, God! It's not me . . . Faina! Don't pay any attention to all this! Don't believe her, my dear!"

On the next day, Faina submitted a report on these happenings to the Leningrad Gas Party Committee and also to the Housing Office, supplying Naum and Lily's co-workers with many hours of amusement. A Party member since 1962, Borenboim got a stiff lecture and was ordered to make peace with his wife, but Faina was in a frenzy. She petitioned for divorce. Naum went to stay with a friend, his wife went to stay with her sister, and they both began intensive negotiations on two new living spaces. Lily, shaken and fearful of universal condemnation, took off for a month at her own expense and slipped away to the Crimea.

We had not yet recovered from the debacle caused by Faina when something else happened that managed to upstage Naum's dramatic performance. Senka Roof and Vasili Bochkin . . . But here the Bochkin family should be properly introduced.

Vasili Bochkin, a heavy-jowled and darkly hairy man who might have had a bit of gypsy blood in him, was as a rule seriously drunk four days of each week. Delicate hints to the effect that it might not be bad to dry out sent him into a frenzy.

"I'm not a problem drinker—I just drink the normal amount," he would roar at his wife, the meekest of women, Lyubov, whom we nicknamed Lyubanya the Dove. "Did you understand that? Do you understand the difference between an alcoholic and a drunk? A drunk, that's what I am, get it? I drink for the joy of it, to express my soul!"

At the time of the events described here, Vasili Bochkin worked as a plumber in the Karl Marx Candy Factory. The sweet, pungent smell of chocolate always hung about him. Lyubov, a worker at the Red Triangle Tire Factory, always smelled of rubber. She was a quality inspector of galoshes.

The couple lived on her wages; Vasili contributed his to the liquor department of the corner grocery. Whenever Bochkin felt that his soul was still not sufficiently expressed, he would try to wheedle money out of his wife. Once in a while she would say no to him and then Vasili would beat her till she was half dead. We would call the police, but in the morning Lyubov would powder her shiners and hurry to the police station to beg to have her treasure released.

Then it happened that she became pregnant, quite unexpectedly. The coming child changed her dove's world view, and she went to the candy factory to demand that Bochkin's salary not be given to him directly. For Vasili this loss of independence was a hard blow.

"Are you a man or a rag to wipe the floor with?" his friend Senka Roof baited him. "She'll make you into a laughing-stock."

Vasili made a scene, managed to get three roubles out of Lyubanya and disappeared for twenty-four hours. And then, just after the fall of the Borenboim family . . . But the story was to be heard in Vasili's own words.

Under cross examination he told it like this.

"I felt upset that day as I was leaving work. I thought if I didn't get something to drink I'd die. My nerves were on end. A human being feels like that sometimes. And I didn't have a kopek in my pocket, and there was nowhere I could get any money."

Vasili glanced at the investigator, who nodded his head sympathetically.

"So I dragged myself home and my wife isn't there yet. I dig around in the cupboard, under the mattress, go through all the dressers—nothing. I couldn't figure out where she was hiding it. And there was no one to borrow from. Naum and Faina had split up, and that bitch in heat, excuse the expression, Lilia Pavlovna, had gone off to the south. My condition, Citizen Investigator, really stank, I couldn't see

143

straight, my head was splitting, my throat felt dry and nothing but blurry faces around me. And that sonofabitch Senka, excuse me, Semyon Prokofievich, hadn't got back yet from work, and all my hopes were pinned on him.

"Then Lyuba comes home, nasty as a witch. It's her, so pregnant you wouldn't know her right off, not a hello or goodbye from her. She throws her purse on the bed and goes into the kitchen. I, of course, turn her handbag inside out, with no results. In a minute she's back from the kitchen and she says, to quote her exactly, 'I'm just going down the block for some bread and then we'll eat.'

"I say to her, 'Wait, Lyuba, I feel sick to my stomach.'"

"'Don't drink so much,' she says and slams the door. I run after her down the stairs. 'Lyuba,' I say, 'be honorable, fork over three roubles!' I remember I even put my arm around her. But she pulled away, her eyes all crazy, and said, 'You go to hell,' and she even used bad language at me.

"'Lyuba,' I say, 'what's come over you? In the near-off past you never used to talk to me like that. For the last time I'm begging you, if not I don't know what I'll do to myself . . .'"

"So you threatened her?" the investigator interrupted for the first time.

"No, I threatened myself, not her! And she says, 'Do what you like, go drown or hang yourself.'

"I go back to our room like a beaten dog. So, I think, that bitch, going on like that. 'Hang yourself,' she says. And if I did, I'd like to see how she's going to bring up the kid without a father."

The picture of the fatherless child upset Vasili so much that he sobbed, and the investigator hurried to him with a glass of water.

"To tell the truth, I wasn't intending to hang myself entirely, but just enough to make the point. I'm not a mon-

144

ster, after all, to leave a kid without a father. I just decided to teach Lyuba a lesson and give her a little scare. I took a rope, wound it around my neck and then under my arms and put my jacket over it so she wouldn't see it. There was no good hook in the room, but there were three good ones in the bathroom for the clothes lines. I pick the strongest-looking one and slip the noose around my neck and climb onto the edge of the tub and wait for the front door to slam. The only thing I was afraid of was falling in the tub, because there was all this underwear soaking in it. Suddenly I hear her come in. I jump off and hang there. The rope scrapes my neck a little, but nothing serious—I can manage, hanging there. I pretend to be dead, roll back my eyes, stick out my tongue. Now, I think she'll poke her nose in here and I'll get a look at her . . .

"I hear footsteps coming down the hall. Just as I plan, they come to the bathroom. Then I see out of the corner of my eye that it's not Lyuba who walks in but my best friend, Senka Roof. He stares at me, his eyes bugging out of his head. Hell, I think, the whole thing is ruined. He's bound to yell like a madman and spoil the effect. I even closed my eyes tight. But that's not what happens. Senka Roof goes and hooks the door shut and then comes over to me. Imagine, Citizen Investigator, Roof begins turning my pockets inside out. He starts groping around in my jacket and pants pockets. It even tickles. Then he grabs my hand and takes my watch off. It was a present from my mother, and I," here Vasili's voice trembled, "I never, no matter how much I needed money, ever even thought of selling it. So I got so furious, so outraged—this man, you understand, is supposed to be my friend, and him robbing a hanged man blind—that I kicked Roof in the stomach with my foot. And he has to go and die of fright on me . . ."

All of this happened at five o'clock one afternoon. Those of us at home suddenly heard an agonizing cry and the sound of a falling body coming from the bathroom. Lyubov Bochkin led the rush to the bathroom door and began to tug at it but it was hooked shut. She tugged harder. Vasili Bochkin was swinging on a hook, trying to reach the edge of the bathtub with his feet, while Senka Roof lay on the floor, wheezing, with Bochkin's watch clutched in his hand.

The ambulance arrived with lightening speed, but it was too late. Senka Roof never regained consciousness and died of a heart attack on the way to the hospital.

And that was when silence finally ruled in our apartment. The Borenboims were nowhere to be seen, Lily Kuzina was sitting out the scandal in Alushta. Senka Roof was no more. Vasili Bochkin was being examined by experts on the criminally insane. Dove-like Lyuba had gone to her mother's on compulsory leave. For the first time in thirty years we got as close as we could get to eternal peace.

Contentment

Vahe Vahian
Translated by Diana Der Hovanessian

That beautiful but tragic heroine, Happiness,
escaped my grasp. I pursued as she fled.
We shipwrecked on stones and I bled
and wore bruises instead of her kiss.

In dark cities, on sunny streets up and down
in my own spirit and in concrete things
I searched. But the quest, yearning,
remained all I ever found.

Perhaps she was a visitor from another star,
a burst of light that opens flowers in the dark.
Not for a moment was I granted the grace

of seeing her; but met in her place
the black bird constantly pecking my heart
while I sought the peace of her embrace.

The Armenian Language is the Home of the Armenian

Moushegh Ishkhan

Translated by Diana Der Hovanessian

The Armenian language is the home
and haven where the wanderer can own
roof and wall and nourishment.
He can enter to find love and pride,
locking the hyena and the storm outside.
For centuries its architects have toiled
to give its ceilings height.
How many peasants working
day and night have kept
its cupboards full, lamps lit, ovens hot.
Always rejuvenated, always old, it lasts
century to century on the path
where every Armenian can find it when he's lost
in the wilderness of his future, or his past.

To You

Eghivart
Translated by Diana Der Hovanessian

Like the wanderer
with the fires of his heart
exhausted, I come to you.
Home, like the terrified boy running
to his mother through the dark
with outstretched arms.

For Years I have been climbing
over hills waiting for the sky
to open and pour on my head.
But it spilled life's wine
into the desert sands.
Only you, living Bread,
can satisfy my hunger and need.

The Apricot Tree

Harout Gosdantian
Translated by Diana Der Hovanessian

Do you know the one word
that holds the beauty of the world,
a whole world of color,
a kaleidoscope of summer,
and inexpressible magic?

You would, if you had seen
that tree blossoming.
Not any tree, but the apricot
budding like Semiramis' breasts,
and greener than the willows in Babylon.

Epigrams

Harout Gosdantian
Translated by Diana Der Hovanessian

You want someone
to dry your tears?
You should have prepared
the handkerchief
last year.

No flower keeps its fragrance,
not the hardiest, nor the strongest.
The odor of the healing herb
lasts longest.

Your eyes close for the favor
of the sweet, first kiss.
And the stolen kiss's flavor?
There's no adjective for this!

Without Memories

Harout Gostantian
Translated by Diana Der Hovanessian

Deep feelings sometimes rush out
in the form of sad tunes.

I enter "Ani"
that old, run-down restaurant
where along the wall, the customers
sit, a bas-relief
of proud suffering faces telling
a cruel past while the chef
calmly recommends lentils and rice
offers also (I can charge it)
cheese, bread and wine.
I too am one of the transported
statues in this strange museum.

Centuries pass quickly.
Twenty years, gone like a day
while we breathe in this different sky
and sun, singing, "Hayasdan."
But hours pass too quickly,
"By the Arax Shores."

We walk, reaching Saint-Michel
and in our continuous anxiety
point out Montparnasse.
We never reach anywhere.

We are still here.
The cranes are still flying.
The cranes are still calling.
Call, Groong, call, crane, while spring calls.
It is spring here.
Memory can bring back a thousand springs.
But I forget the name of that blonde Norwegian,
white as a snow flower,
when the cranes of home call.

In Montparnasse
Balzac stands with me and we enjoy
the rain. He says:
"Go and have a coffee. Perhaps
you can remember more. Or forget
more."

Behind me dancers lean against each other
tipsily.
The wise man says, "We shall find
the road again. It always leads East,
slightly south.
Along its way are springs for us,
the thirsty. Deserts that are pastures."

The dancers stomp now.
Savage fevers liven their tempo.
Drums insist on more passion.
The lights go off.

"We shall see beyond the distance
into the night that is a morning
where beauty is a constant."

The dancers grow more agitated
enraged, almost violent,
in frenzied couplings.

"We shall hear the gentle flutes,
and the immensity shall be bridged."
The saxophone and horns shout.
The dancers vibrate.

I know a song, old as the mountains -
sun-scorched by longing sadness,
I am the torrent in the ravine
which has run dry.
I am the deep memories of
the stream without rein,
the formless direction of floods.
And here is the dry summer
thirsty for rain.

Oath to Ararat

Antranik Zaroukian
Translated by Diana Der Hovanessian

We will reach your sacred peak
once the barrage of bombs subsides,
once the blood seas resign themselves
to being the color of blood,
once the butchered dove of peace
returns from the holocaust
with his olive branch.
We will reach that summit.

From every city, by-road and field
from every gutter and corner of exile,
watch us gather, adding one to one
and rank to rank, to storm our father's dream.
And watch the black walls with which
fate has barricaded us
shatter.

The ache of our hearts will lead us
like a trumpet call,
to our lands and water.
Let the sun collapse;
let the road lead through hell,
we will reach your peak.

Look at our numbers, swelling rank on rank
brave and burning.
Look at our hunger reaching toward you
with the grasp and reach of Vahakn.
Look at our souls clean as your snows.
And our will, hard as your stones.
God of granite!
Holy mountain!
Believe us that we can,
that we shall reach your peak!

Let It be Light

Antranik Zaroukian
Translated by Diana Der Hovanessian

Let it rest lightly,
if it can,
this foreign soil.
Let it grow pity like a bloom.
Although once you said
even the air in a foreign land
is heavy and cuts the lungs.

Let it be light,
this handful of earth
I throw against the coffin,
my last debt and your newest
wound.

Without a fatherland
the landless find
all brown earth an insult,
all soil rootless.
The exile is a stranger
even to his grave.

Yesterday you wrestled luck
boot to boot. The Armenian's lot
is to fight for his lost land.
Even after death. Now fight
this soil over you. Hold it
lightly and away from your face.

Four Prisoners of War

. . . . In the course of their interrogation, prior to their transfer to the detention camp of Antikalamos (as per Emergency Law 509 against sedition and armed insurrection), four of the prisoners made the following statements, which are hereby appended for inclusion in their files.

Kavalla Stockade
23 December 1949

(Signed and stamped)
D. M. Koliopoulos
Ensign, Royal Hellenic Navy

STAMATIS X. (No surname) Age 13

"Before I joined the guerrillas, or 'bandits,' as you called them, I used to steal a lot. I stole from the Germans and the Italians, and later on from the English too, and when they caught me I lied or joked about it, and the Greeks used to tell me, 'Don't you have any pride left?' and I thought they said 'bread,' so I answered, 'No, can't you tell?' And when I was ten I borrowed money from other kids and never returned it, and everybody in my hometown whispered to everybody else, 'Watch out for Stamatis, he makes things disappear before your eyes.' Even my own parents didn't trust me, and my father got tired of beating me and one day he kicked me out of the house, and that's how I didn't get killed with my parents when a shell blew up our house. Next I had to leave town because everyone got to know me too well and stealing was difficult. After that I went around the country with a gang of kids my age. Every morning we split into groups of three and went out begging and stealing, and in the evening we divided the loot and had a good time. That way I made some friends too. Except pretty soon I started to cheat on them, and they kicked me out, saying, 'There ought to be honesty at least among crooks.' After that I wandered about in the mountains, pretending to be lost, and to be a sympathizer of the guerrillas, so I could steal from them also, but they caught me in the act and put me in quarantine. For three days and nights they didn't talk to me or give me any food or water, and I thought to myself, 'This is it, Stamatis, prepare to meet your makers,' by which I meant my father and mother, because I thought that was the end, the noose at the end of the rope. But on the fourth day Capetan Porphyris brought me some food and water, and as I ate I started to cry. Capetan Porphyris said anyone who stole for his bread ought to weep when he ate it. But that was the last time I cried while I ate because I never stole again. Capetan Porphyris said that when the war was over there'd be no place for crooks anymore, and I believed him, but look what happened: the crooks won the war! At any rate, I asked Capetan Porphyris for work, because I didn't want to fight, what sort of work I could do, and he said, 'How about feeding the mules? it's easier than stealing.' So that's what I did, and I didn't have to steal anymore. After Grammos fell, when we were still hiding in the cave, I knew that we'd run out of food before the winter, and I ate less, giving half of my ration to the little ones and to the sick, because for years I'd eaten bread that belonged to others. And many weeks went by without food whatever, so I suppose I must be about even by now."

159

OHANES NAZARIAN, age 12

"My grandfather was an Armenian refugee from Anatolia, and he knew many stories, a different one for each occasion, but I always liked this one about Nastradin Hodja, who was a famous sage throughout Turkey: One summer noon Nastradin was resting in the shade of a tall hazel nut tree, like those growing around Grammos, and next to him was a pumpkin patch. Nastradin looked up at the hazel nuts and down at the pumpkins, and scratching his white beard he said, 'Allah, you've created everything with much care and consideration, with much wisdom, but here I'm afraid there's a flaw. Why should a tall tree like this make such a tiny fruit as the hazel nut, and this small plant make such a huge fruit as the pumpkin? it just doesn't follow.' For some time Nastradin gazed at the hazel nuts up high and the pumpkins down by his feet, wondering whether or not Allah would ever answer his question, when a tiny hazel nut fell from its branch and hit him right on the head. That was Allah's answer to his question. Can you imagine what would have happened to Nastradin's head if the hazel nuts were as big as pumpkins? Well, I don't remember the occasion of grandfather's telling this story, but I think during the battles of Grammos the hazel nuts that fell on our heads were as big as pumpkins, because Allah had closed down his shop there and moved to Athens where the dollars were."

MARTIS X. (No surname), age 8

"One day when I was little, just before I started to walk, my brother Nionios, who was five, saw the village vet searing a horse's knee with a red hot iron, and he asked him why he was doing that. The vet said that the horse had a problem walking, because there were fluids inside its knee, and when the water was burnt out the horse was going to walk all right again. In the morning my parents went to the field, and my brother Nionios heated up the tongs in our fireplace until they were red hot, and he burned my knees so I could quit crawling and start to walk. My brother wanted to help me but he didn't know how, and it took me even longer to walk upright because of the burns, and even now my knees hurt and I limp a little when there's a change in the weather. So we thought maybe the guerrillas could help us, but they didn't know any better, and now we're burnt, and you haven't finished heating up your tongs yet . . . So what I want to say is, don't try to help us . . . let us be . . . why don't you just leave us alone."

TIMOS OR TIMON, ALIAS AGAMEMNON X, age 12

"I swear to tell the truth. When I was on the Mountain I had a reputation for telling tall stories, and some of the guerrillas even called me a liar, but I never told a lie, and now, because of the guerrillas, I'm accused of having been a bandit. What can I say? The guerrillas took me away in order to save me from the bombs, but they didn't ask my family, and they didn't pay attention to me when I was screaming that I didn't want to be saved. But whenever they paid attention to me, they ended up calling me a liar. Once I saw a giant in a cave. He didn't eat up people like Cyclops, he didn't even fight in the war. He just milked his sheep for cheese and yogurt, and he made pancakes for breakfast: large pancakes that he served with fresh cream and grape syrup. When I told what I'd seen, everybody

161

laughed. 'Sure,' they said. 'What else did the giant do? did he make rice pudding too? did he make baklava?' If you tell them about a good giant they never take you seriously. So today I am not going to say anything about giants, but about little, very little people: there is this old-time bazaar somewhere in the Orient, where all kinds of people from all over the world gather to trade horses and camels, and to sell food, clothes, rugs—you name it. There are gypsies, money exchangers, beggars, magicians, vagabonds, pickpockets, and other miracle-workers turning flint into diamonds, brass into gold, and small portions of fish and wine into enough food and drink to entertain an army. To make a long story short, there's also a character there who works with wood. Yes, wood. He'd whittle odd pieces of wood with his pocket-knife, turning out all sorts of little wild beasts: lions, panthers, crocodiles and such, that come to life as soon as he finishes them. Don't say that's impossible, because I myself happened to be there once, and I saw it with my own eyes. And the other thing I saw was that those beasts were hungry and dangerous, so I asked their maker to tell me what they fed on. 'Here,' he said, and taking a few more pieces of wood, he started whittling away, and before I knew it he came up with these funny little people, who also came to life as soon as he'd finished them. 'They come free,' he said. And when I looked at them closely, I saw that they were the poor and the homeless, people without a country, refugees and exiles, men, women, and children who have nothing on earth, and the heaven has nothing for them. Little people like us. Food for the lions. 'They come free,' he said to me. And he said, 'Where are *you* from? have I seen you someplace before? are you from around here or what?'"

162

Contributors' Notes

MARGUERITE GUZMAN BOUVARD

Marguerite Guzman Bouvard was born in Trieste, Italy. She received an M.A. in Creative Writing from Boston University and a Ph.D. in Political Science from Harvard University. She has been Poet-in-Residence at the University of Maryland and has taught poetry at the Radcliffe Seminars. At Regis College, she is professor of Political Science and conducts poetry workshops. In addition to several books in Political Science, she has written a book of poems, "Journeys Over Water," which won the Quarterly Review of Literature contest in 1982. She has been a fellow at the Bunting Institute, at Yaddo, the MacDowell Colony, the Virginia Center for the Creative Arts, and the Ragdale Foundation, and has had a scholarship in poetry from the Bread Loaf Writers' Conference.

DENIS BRUTUS

Denis Brutus was born in Salisbury, Zimbabwe of South African parents, and educated in South Africa. While a university student, he began his lifelong struggle against Apartheid. His protests led to his persecution and a series of imprisonments. He was arrested in 1963 and escaped. In 1965 he was shot on a Johannesburg street and then sent to Robbens Island. In 1965 he was placed under house arrest and a year later, exiled. Since that time, he founded and headed the South African Non-Racial Olympic Committee which has been successful in barring South Africa from the Olympic Games. He is now professor of English at Northwestern University. He is the author of nine books, all of them banned in South Africa.

DIANA DER HOVANESSIAN

Diana Der Hovanessian was born in Worcester, Massachusetts and educated at Boston University and Harvard. She is author of, "How to Choose Your Past," and the translator and co-editor of four books of Armenian poetry including the prize-winning "Anthology of Armenian Poetry." She is president of the New England Poetry Club and works as a poet in the Massachusetts schools.

EGHIVART is the nom de plume of the Patriarch of Jerusalem, Archbishop Eghishe Derderian. He was born in Van, Armenia. He lost his parents and was deported during the massacres. Eghivart obtained his formal education at the Armenian seminary in Jerusalem. He has published several volumes of poetry.

HAROUT GOSDANTIAN was born in Booshir, Iran and lived in India and England until settling in France. He has published two books of poems, "The Wisdom of Days," and "With Poetry."

MOUSHEGH ISHKHAN was orphaned by the Turkish massacres of the Armenians when he was two. He was educated in Beirut where he now teaches at the Jemaran School. He is the author of books of poems, plays, novels and a series of textbooks on Armenian literature.

VAHE VAHIAN was born in Gurin, Turkey and deported during the massacres to Aleppo, Syria. He was raised and educated in Beirut where he is now a professor. He is well known as a poet, editor and educator. He was recently honored by the Soviet Armenian government for his contributions to Armenian literature in the diaspora.

ANTRANIG ZAROUKIAN was born in Gurin, Turkey and orphaned by the Turkish massacre of Armenians. He grew up in Aleppo, Syria. He has written four novels and also books of poetry. He lives in Beirut where he is a literary critic, a journalist and edits a literary weekly.

ELZBIETA ETTINGER

Elzbieta Ettinger was born, raised and educated in Poland. A free-lance writer until 1967, she has published essays, translations and literary criticism in Polish journals and magazines. She came to the United States in the late sixties and was a senior fellow at the Bunting Institute from 1969 to 1973. She is an associate professor at the Massachusetts Institute of Technology and teaches in the writing program. She is author of a novel, "Kindergarten," and of "Comrade and Lover: Rosa Luxembourg's Letters to Leo Jogiches."

STRATIS HAVIARAS

Stratis Haviaras was born in Greece and came to the United States in 1967. He lives in Cambridge, Massachusetts where he has been an editor of Arion's Dolphin, a literary magazine, and of "The Poet's Voice," a collection on tape of major American poets reading their work. His works include, "Crossing the River Twice," a book of poems, and two novels "When the Tree Sings," and "The Heroic Age." He is also the author of four books of poetry written in Greek. He works as a librarian at Harvard University.

IFEANYI MENKITI

Ifeanyi Menkiti was born in Onitsha, Nigeria, and has lived in California, New York, and Massachusetts. He received his Ph.D from Harvard University and is currently a professor of philosophy at Wellesley College. His books of poems include, "Affirmations," and "The Jubilation of Falling Bodies." He has received fellowships in poetry from the National Endowment for the Arts and the Massachusetts Arts and Humanities Foundation.

ALI MORAD FADAIE-NIA

Ali Morad Fadaie-Nia was born in Bibian, Iran and came to the United States in 1977. In Iran, he has published several novels and collections of short stories. He lives in New York City.

FELIX MORRISSEAU-LEROY

Felix Morrisseau-Leroy was born in Grand-Gosier, Haiti and has degrees from the University of Port-Au-Prince, Columbia, New York City College and the New School of Social Research. He was exiled in 1959 and since then has lived in Africa and the United States. In Ghana, he served as national organiser of drama and literature at the Arts Council, and in Senegal, as Technical Adviser of the Senegalese Federation of People's Theater. He currently lives in Miami, Florida where he writes and produces plays in Creole. He has written numerous books of poetry, novels, and plays including "Ravinodyab", "Plenitudes", "Recolte", "Diacoute I", "Antigone en Creole". His works have been translated into French, English, Spanish, German, Russian, Fanti, Twi, and Wolof, and his plays have been performed around the world. Although he is multilingual, Felix Morrisseau-Leroy prefers to write in Creole, because he wishes "to express the deepest feelings, emotions and aspirations of the people for whom he claims to be a mere scribe."

ROSE MOSS

Rose Moss was born and raised in South Africa. She came to the United States in 1964 and taught creative writing at Wellesley College from 1972 to 1982. She has published two novels, "The Family Reunion," and "The Terrorist," as well as short stories, articles and poems. She has been a fellow at Yaddo, the Mac-Dowell Colony and the Ossabaw Island Project. She recently acquired an MBA and consults on issues of innovation, new technology and Artificial Intelligence.

LUDMILA SHTERN

Ludmila Shtern was born in Leningrad where she attended school and received the Ph.D in Geology. While in the Soviet Union, she was a professor of geology. However, she was unable to publish her short stories because of their revelations of the difficulties of daily life in the Soviet Union. She came to the United States in 1976. Her novels have been translated into several languages and one novel, "Petersburg University," was serialized in the British Broadcasting Corporation's broadcasts to the Soviet Union. Her stories have appeared in Pequod, Story, The Washington Post, and The New Russian Word.

TIBOR TOLLAS

Tibor Tollas was born in Nagybarca, Hungary and studied at the Ludovika Academy Officers School. He was an army officer during World War II and was seriously wounded. In 1947, he was arrested on false charges and spent nine years as a political prisoner in various jails and forced labor camps. In the maximum security prison of Vac, he collected the first Hungarian Samisdat writings, 12 handwritten booklets, smuggled from cell to cell and hidden in cracks. Three copies made their way to the West and became known as "The Herbgarden," published in Vienna in 1957. During the political thaw of 1956, he was released and fought in the Hungarian Revolution. He then escaped to the West. He lives in Munich where he edits "The Hungarian Guardian," a political and literary journal. He is author of five books of poetry.

VÕ PHIẾN

Vo Phien is the pen name of Doan The Nhon. He was born in Binh Dinh, Vietnam and came to the United States in 1975. In Vietnam, he was professor of literature at Hoa Hoa University and Phuon Nam University, and founder and manager of the

Thoi Moi publishing company. He was also a journalist and member of the Council for Cultural and Educational Affairs between 1970 and 1974. He is a winner of the Vietnamese National Literary prize and author of 29 works. Currently he lives in California where he is the founder and editor in chief of Van Hoc Nghe Thuat, a Vietnamese language literary journal. He is a frequent contributor to Vietnamese magazines.

ARMANDO VALLADARES

Armando Valladares was born in Pinar del Rio, Cuba, and attended the National School of the Arts in Havana. At the age of 23, he was arrested for speaking out against communism, refusing to join the militia or to put on a uniform. He was charged with "crimes against the powers of the states," and with being "a potential enemy of the revolution." He spent 22 years in prison: six years on "Devil's Island", 7 years in the Spanish colonial fortress of La Cabana, 4 years in the Boniato prison, and 5 years in Combinado des Este, in Havana.

A rebellious prisoner of deep Christian and political convictions, he refused the rehabilitation programs and consequently was subjected to physical and psychological torture. When the government wanted to force the rebellious prisoners to wear the uniform of common deliquents, Valladares refused. For many years he was held in isolation, without clothing, visitation rights or medical assistance. In 1974, Valladares was paralyzed with polyneuritis after being deprived of food for 46 days.

It was then that he wrote his first book "From My Wheel Chair," followed by "Prisoner of Castro", and "The Heart in Which I Live." They were smuggled out of prison and published by his wife Marta. These books were translated into several languages and made him known around the world. He was made a "prisoner of conscience," by Amnesty International. The Pen Club of France and Sweden made him an honorary member, and France granted him the Libertad award in 1980. Appeals for his release came from U.S. senators, the presidents of Venezuela and Mexico, the International Red Cross, the Inter-American

Commission on Human Rights, and Amnesty International. After a petition submitted by Marta Valladares and Fernando Arrabal to the French President Mitterand, the lobbying proved effective. Valladares was released in 1982 following Mitterand's intervention.

With Vladimir Bukovsky, the Soviet dissident, he founded the International Resistance, an organization made up of politicians, journalists, intellectuals and organizations that fight totalitarianism throughout the world, and the violations of human rights whether of the left or the right.

Valladares now lives in Madrid. His third book of poems, "The Caverns of Silence," is forthcoming. Currently, he is working on his memoirs.

This book was set in Caledonia at Graphic Composition, Athens, Georgia and printed on acid-free paper at Malloy Lithography, Ann Arbor, Michigan.

Rowan Tree Press
124 Chestnut Street
Boston, Massachusetts 02108

DATE DUE
